MEMORIES

OF HAPPY DAYS

MEMORIES

OF

HAPPY DAYS

*

JULIAN GREEN

*

GREENWOOD PRESS, PUBLISHERS
NEW YORK

To my cousin NAN WILLIAMS,
who made it possible for
me to write this book

Two years have now gone by since France fell, but I do not think that the meaning of such an event can yet be perfectly understood. There is something in many of us which refuses to contemplate a world in which France would no longer hold her accustomed place. She was and still remains indispensable to the civilization of the white race. She did not achieve supremacy by brute force — her neighbor did that, to the detriment of the whole world — but what France did achieve in the field of culture, century after century, no armies in the world can completely wrest from her, neither can any nation, however powerful, boast spiritual superiority over Germany's proud and unhappy victim. Caliban may succeed in overcoming Prospero by treachery and physical strength, but this can only mean that Caliban has more cunning and is physically stronger than Prospero, and can mean little else. And Caliban's real victim, if he does succeed in overcoming Prospero, is Caliban, as we shall see if the curse of German domination is not lifted from Europe.

I do not say that Germany is Caliban and that France is

Prospero, but I do say that the lowest ambitions of humanity have found expression in the group of Germans now leading their country and the whole Continent to chaos. The existence of great and irreplaceable things in our world is being threatened by these unconscious barbarians who fail to realize that a victory of one part of Europe over the other makes Europe the principal loser. Such is human solidarity that wars of conquest can never be won; they must forever and tragically be lost, and lost by all.

With all her human failings, France has that quality of greatness which can never be taken from her by misfortune. It may now be obscured by defeat in the eyes of those who judge superficially, but it is hers still in spite of the degrading presence of the Nazi army on her soil. She has learned to her grief that her greatness is no longer military greatness. Military greatness is, after all, the most primitive form of greatness, and France, like all highly civilized nations, was in the process of outgrowing it. Her genius lay elsewhere than in war, neither could she quite bring herself to believe that civilization had to be defended by mechanized armies and that spiritual ends could be achieved by high explosive bombs. In this she woefully lacked wisdom. The disastrous Maginot Line was the only solution she could find to a problem which did not really interest her. Very pathetic, in the view of what happened later, are the inscriptions on the new Trocadéro buildings overlooking

viii

the Seine. At the time when Germany was making the weapons with which to kill her, France was covering the walls of a marble palace with the beautiful abstract words of a poet. In the soft light of the Paris sky, beloved of so many painters, how often have my eyes read the harmonious sentences which spoke not of military strength, but of intelligence and beauty, lines which might have earned praise from Plato but could hardly be understood by the well-groomed and well-armed toughs who blinked at them through their German monocles, in June 1940.

The book which I am about to send to my publishers I offer as an affectionate tribute to the France I shall forever love and admire. To a large extent, this book is an account of my childhood and the early part of my youth, but as a matter of fact it differs somewhat from the book I had in mind when I sat down to write the first page. It was then my intention to try to express my conception of France and what France stood for, but on further consideration of that subject, it occurred to me that I could best show what I owed to France by calling up the memories of all the happy days I had spent under her kindly and generous care; at the same time I thought it might perhaps be a suitable way of thanking that great and good person.

The first pages of the book were written a few days after my arrival in this country. I, like hundreds of thousands of other people, was still feeling the effects of the stunning

blow we had received and I could think of no better way of
dulling the pain of this wound than immediately setting to
work. France was, of course, forever in my mind. I did not
want to forget her, I wanted, on the contrary, to find her
again, not as I had seen her a few weeks before, beaten and
humiliated, but as I had known her all my life, with a smile
on her beautiful face.

When I was a child, owing to my misapprehension of
a picture in a history book, I got it into my head that France
was a real person, a woman with a crown which she doffed
at certain times to wear a Phrygian cap, and one of my main
sources of worry was that, sooner or later, this person with
whom I was in love would grow old and eventually die.
Hence the strange questions I used to ask my mother:
"How old is France? Is she twenty, or thirty? Do you think
she will live a long time?" So deeply embedded in my
mind was this idea that, even as a full grown man, I could
never quite get rid of it, neither did I really want to get rid
of it, because it seemed to me that somehow it contained
more truth, more hidden truth, than I was able to realize
as a child.

I believe that if we think of a country as a mass of human beings obeying this or that directive which they re-
ceive at the hands of a political body called the government,
we are apt to form an incomplete and unsatisfactory idea
of that country's personality which we somehow confuse

with the personality of the men who are at its head. That is why cartoonists seem to me to come nearer to the truth, in a clumsy way, when they depict nations as people. Nations are people and when we think of them as people they become startlingly real. If we think of France as a person we love being reviled and spat upon by the Nazis, her case becomes infinitely more pathetic. We know that she has been unwise, that her mistakes have been very numerous, that she is far from perfect, but she knows that too, better than any one; and the fact remains that in spite of her present humiliation, she is greatly superior to her foe and spiritually she towers above him from the cross to which he has nailed her.

What is going to happen to her, we cannot tell. We know that she will not die, because a spirit does not die and she is, essentially, a spirit, but her physical life is threatened and her physical life is as precious to many of us as the life of a mother. We need her presence. Her place cannot be filled by other nations. It is impossible that she will disappear, but if she did, a great many reasons for being attached to this life would disappear with her. She has given us more than we know, she has made this world richer and more beautiful for millions of men and women; if she ever went, we might not cease to live, but we should be poorer and something in us would die. That, however, will not happen.

Whatever my intentions were when I began my book, I never wanted it to be a sad book. Throughout her long history, France has showed us that she knew how to smile in her most tragic hours and I have tried to profit by her example. A smile does not always mean that the heart has stopped aching, it often indicates that hope is still there, in spite of everything.

MEMORIES

OF HAPPY DAYS

CHAPTER ONE

Both my parents were Southerners. My mother came from Savannah, Georgia, and my father from Prince William County, Virginia. When my mother felt combative, she would taunt my father with the fact that Virginia was the last state to secede and my elder sisters would say: "There they go again!" The war was usually fought around the dining-room table, calf-bound volumes of the Confederate Papers being brought out to prove or disprove hotly disputed points which we children missed more often than not. I suppose, however, that I am going too fast and that I should start at the beginning.

Around 1895, my parents moved from Savannah where they had been married to Le Havre, in Normandy, where my father had been offered a position as European agent for the Southern Cotton Oil Company. They did not stay there very long; in 1898 they moved to Paris. Our family furniture, which had come all the way from Savannah, accompanied them by what the French call *petite vitesse,* a term which George Du Maurier, in *Trilby,* translates as "little quickness," and a good phrase when all is considered. This furniture was an object of amazement for my parents' Parisian friends who had never seen anything like it: curly armchairs, long, sinuous sofas with voluptuous ante-bellum curves, to the French eye a spectacle of horror, but according to our standards, masterpieces of good taste. We revelled in the thought of sitting on rosewood chairs and I suppose that the name of the wood pleased us as much as did the clusters of little flowers which were carved on the slanting backs.

As a matter of fact, this furniture which had been made for my grandfather around 1850 must have looked very strange and out of place in our flat, at number 4 rue Rhumkorff. The low-ceilinged rooms had never sheltered anything but reasonable tables and chairs of the Louis XVI type or perhaps Empire and Louis-Philippe of the most conservative description, whereas our drawing-room chairs, for instance, had something flighty and irresponsible about them and looked as if they were about to get up in some curious way and waltz. On the other hand, the dining-room chairs, which were made of solid mahogany and covered with dark green leather, had a heavy, serious, business-like appearance somewhat alleviated by the fact that the legs looked like nothing else in the world but fat ladies' legs coming out of frilled pantalets. We fancied them inordinately and claimed that there was nothing like them in France, a statement which has justly remained undisputed to this day.

I was born on the sixth of September 1900, in the rue Rhumkorff, Paris, but our street was so near the gates of the city that, had my parents lived a few hundred yards further west, it could not be my boast today that I am a Parisian by birth as well as an American citizen. Neither do I mean that I was naturalized an American: I am American born, not made.

The rue Rhumkorff left no impression on my mind whatever, but I heard it referred to in later years with much shaking of heads as the place where my parents had their greatest financial struggle. I did not like the name of the street, which sounded like someone coughing, and I always connected it with the gloom of poverty, but some time ago I made a trip to that distant part of Paris and found our house better looking than I had thought, small in size and plain in design, but clean and, as people say, respectable though the neighborhood was said to be rowdy.

In 1903, we moved to Passy and became so attached to that part of Paris that we lived there for thirty-five years. Passy is that part of the city which adjoins the Bois de Boulogne, where parents take their children to play on the lawns or ride on the merry-go-rounds in the daytime and where scenes less innocent in character take place after

3

dark. Of this we knew and suspected nothing, to be sure, and found the Bois a little tedious, because once you were there you had to play, whether you felt like it or not, and we much preferred walking up and down the rue de Passy with our mother and looking at the shops.

Our house in the rue de Passy is so filled with memories of happiness that I hope to be forgiven if I enlarge a little on the subject. The flat we lived in was on the third floor, with low ceilings and rather dark rooms. There was an old-fashioned bell-pull at the front door and if you grasped it firmly and agitated it with sufficient energy, you could hear a faint tinkle somewhere at the back of the house, then a sound of footsteps and my mother's high-pitched voice exclaiming: "If it's another bill, I won't pay it!" Children flew in and out of rooms, doors were slammed and finally, after a pause, the door was opened by a dour looking maid with a white apron and a white cap hastily and angrily pinned on the top of her head. White caps, at sea, are indicative of stormy weather. This white cap was the cause of tempestuous arguments between my mother who insisted on its wear by her maids and the latter who invariably rebelled against a time-honored French custom.

The dark hall opened into my parents' bedroom to the right and the drawing room to the left. I am afraid the drawing room would have seemed quite wrong to the editors of *Vogue* or *House and Garden*. For one thing, the furni-

4

ture was ill-assorted and created an effect of confusion, but
I can never think of that room without a feeling of longing
and the hope that in some strange way it may have been
translated to a better world with all the happiness that
went with it. There was an elephantine Chesterfield under
a gas chandelier, and by the door an upright piano of dark
brown wood. My mother's small mahogany desk stood at an
angle near the window with letters sticking out on all sides
like feathers on a bird. Armchairs of various descriptions
were arranged in a semi-circle around the mantelpiece and
seemed to be discussing the holes in the hearth rug. One
of the most peculiar features of this room was that the walls
at one end of it were curved; in consequence, the door by
the piano was rounded so that, when that door was thrown
open, a small boy could easily hide between it and the wall
and frighten whoever came in. I took advantage of this
situation and was considered a bore by my mother's friends
whom I usually chose as my victims.

To frighten others or to frighten myself seemed to be
one of my chief delights as a child. Pouncing suddenly on
my sisters' piano teacher was of course a treat, but I enjoyed
a great deal more the thrill of horror which I invariably got
from peering into my mother's clothespress after having
summoned the Devil to appear. In order to be understood,
I must explain that, according to the firmest of my beliefs,
the Devil lived in my mother's clothespress, a particularly

5

dark and gloomy closet which opened into my parents' bedroom. Invoking the Evil One was a terrifying if simple ceremony. It consisted of throwing the door of the press suddenly wide open and standing back five or six feet for safety's sake. The next thing was to call on the Devil; this requiring a certain amount of intrepidity but threw me into a state of nervous excitement which was, I suppose, a reward in itself. I therefore stood in front of the open door and not once but three times shouted: *"Diable!"* in a somewhat choky voice. The first invocation was bad enough, goodness knows; the second made the whole of my scalp tingle and the third would send me flying out of the room to my mother, who could not understand why I hid my face in her lap with groans of terror. Had she, however, seen what I fancied I saw in the clothespress, she would have been as alarmed as I was, but I am aware that I cannot reasonably hope to be believed when I speak of what I saw in that dreadful closet and how my mother's dresses and my father's suits would begin to stir ever so gently between the second and third invocation, as if someone had been pushing these garments aside in order to come out and, I supposed, leap at me.

Had I been really brave, I should have stayed on, but somehow courage failed me at the very last moment and fear overcame my curiosity. This I always regretted, and promised myself to stay my ground the next time, being

6

particularly anxious to find out what the Devil looked like. Nevertheless, each new attempt ended in the shameful flight I have described, and to this day my conception of the Devil's appearance is based on second-hand information.

Since I have mentioned the supernatural, I may as well confess at this point that we all believed our flat to be haunted, with the exception of my father who refused to entertain what he considered idle and superstitious fears. I have always believed, however, that imaginary evils can be just as troublesome as real ones and that there is often very little difference in the effect they have on the minds of their victims. My parents' room was large, fairly well lighted and cheerful enough in the daytime, with a large window overlooking our landlord's garden, in the middle of which grew a magnificent chestnut tree. In this tree lived a blackbird whose merry whistling entranced me, particularly in the early morning when I lay in bed and watched the light grow brighter just above the drawn curtains. Although I did not suffer from nightly terrors, I always experienced a feeling of relief when the first rays of sunshine crept into our room through the shutters and gave back to everything its familiar appearance, when my father's clothes on a chair stopped looking like a hunchback crouching in a corner and the little white wardrobe no longer took on the aspect of a headless woman dressed in a sheet, with large, square shoulders. Somehow the blackbird's call would help to dispel these silly thoughts.

I may add that I was thankful that my parents' bed stood between mine and the dreaded closet where the Devil had chosen to live, and I knew that no harm could ever befall me so long as my parents were near. This gave me a sense of superiority over my sisters, who slept in other rooms and were not afforded the same protection. In spite of the fact that they were not allowed to mention anything like a ghost in my presence, I soon gathered from their looks and their whisperings that there was something wrong with every room in the house. In one room, as I was told in later years, a severed head was placed every night on the top of a cupboard, between the hours of eleven and twelve. In another room, the one next to my parents', a woman would come regularly and sit at the foot of my youngest sister's bed, for no other reason, I suppose, than to look at her; what made matters worse was the fact that this nocturnal visitor had no face.

It is easy enough to laugh at superstitious fears when one is grown up and knows better than to believe in ghosts. To a nervous child, however, going to bed by candle light with the knowledge that sooner or later this light will have to be extinguished and that some nameless bugbear will then appear in the dark, may be the cause of acute mental suffering with far-reaching consequences. My sister Lucy,

8

who was then in her tenth or twelfth year, was a prey to nightmares which affected very seriously and almost completely shattered her nerves. She it was who saw, or fancied she saw, a woman come into her room and sit on her bed every night, just a few minutes before dawn. My eldest sister who slept in the same room — we were then five children and our flat was none too large — corroborated Lucy's statement concerning the apparition, but all this was put down as nonsense and I fear that much harm resulted from it in Lucy's later years.

It annoyed my father to think that he had rented a comfortable flat for a period of three years and that his children had not spent a week in it before they had, as he phrased it, filled it with spooks. Absolutely nothing could be done about this. The idea of writing to Monsieur Cassagnade, our landlord, was too absurd to be entertained one minute. Imagine complaining to a French landlord that the flat he has let you is haunted! He would have turned you over to an alienist, after having collected the rent.

So my father begged his daughters to be reasonable, adding that he felt sure that startling noises and obnoxious visions would stop by and by, "provided you girls don't pay attention to them." This hopeful view of the situation met with gloomy disapproval, however, and "you girls" went on hearing and seeing exactly what they had heard and seen before. Someone walked up and down the hall

9

most of the night, making the floor creak so loudly that the noise finally awoke such a sound sleeper as my father himself, who took his old-fashioned revolver out of a drawer and left his bed to investigate. Of course he found no one in the hall, and his daughters told him that he was simply not psychic.

After a certain time, there was no more mention of the ghosts. We became used to them and I suppose that they reluctantly accepted our presence in what they, no doubt, considered their own house. From time to time, some reference was made to their doings, and Mary, an expert on such matters, would cast a significant look in my direction so that nothing might be said which I could understand, and then whisper that "*they* had been particularly bad last night." But I understood quite well what was meant. Everybody understood and nobody seemed to care very much, except Lucy.

CHAPTER TWO

Whatever went on at night, our flat in the daytime was as
cheerful as any I have ever lived in. The house must have
been built at the time of Napoleon the First and there was
a fireback in the drawing-room hearth with an imperial
eagle which seemed to move and flap its wings in the glow
of the coals. How often have I watched that eagle and
rolled in front of the hearth on the thin rug, for no other
reason than a sort of animal happiness, an exquisite feeling
of well-being which I seldom experienced after those early
days.

On winter evenings, we would place a cushion on the
floor for my mother, who sat facing the fire with a long
gray woolen shawl around her shoulders and told us stories
about America. We all fought to sit as close to her as possible; but I being the smallest always managed to creep
into her lap, and although I could not understand what
she said I enjoyed listening to the sound of her voice. It
has now been silent for twenty-six years, yet I remember

it as distinctly as if she had just now called me by my name: a clear, high-toned, happy voice.

Over and over again, she would tell us about Savannah where she was born and about the large Tudor house which our grandfather had built in one of the squares, shortly before the War between the States. I have often wondered what picture my mother's words conjured up in her daughters' minds, for the Savannah house, as it was always called, was such an odd mixture of Victorian Gothic and pseudo-Louis XV that it seemed almost impossible to convey an idea of what that venerable building really looked like, particularly to little girls of ten or fourteen who had never set foot in America.

Be that as it may, the Savannah house floated through many conversations like a sort of heavenly Jerusalem, or so it seemed to me when I learned enough English to follow my mother's speech, and I formed such a magnificent idea of that exalted home that very few palaces on earth could have lived up to my expectations; indeed I fear that when I first saw the Savannah house through the critical eyes of nineteen, I felt a slight shock of disappointment. It mattered very little, though; what was really important was that for many years we had lived happily in an imaginary house built of thin air with the stones and mortar of my mother's words.

To us children, America seemed so remote that I sometimes wondered, in a dreamy sort of way, if it wasn't a place my mother had made up for our entertainment. One of my reasons for thinking so was that I could form no mental picture of a country where everything differed so sharply from the rue de Passy as to appear unnatural and sometimes alarming. To think, for instance, that large and deadly snakes were to be found in the woods near the city where my mother had lived, was of course fascinating; but in order to imagine what she meant, I had to picture myself with my *bonne* Lina walking in the Bois de Boulogne and being attacked by a reptile about the size of a boa constrictor. I shuddered at the thought of the dangers my mother had been exposed to and felt happy that our reasonable French snakes were not on the rampage like their American cousins, but lived, I fancied, orderly lives in nice cages at the Jardin des Plantes.

Another story which I preferred neither to believe nor disbelieve but placed on the same level as the tale of Jack and the bean-stalk, was the one about houses more than three times as high as the house we lived in, that is to say, houses with eighteen or twenty floors to them. This, to be sure, was monstrous, but you were at liberty to believe such things although you knew in your heart that they were not so, just as in the case of Jack and the bean-stalk. It was safer, too, not to contradict parents. Nevertheless I secretly refused to admit that a house could be more than five or six stories high, because ours wasn't. I could, of course, pretend that I believed my mother, with the tacit understanding that she no more believed what she said than I did.

This complicated mental process was shattered one day by the arrival of a strange object which, my mother affirmed, had actually come from Savannah. It looked, I thought, like a green walking stick and did not seem to me worthy of the excitement I noticed in every one as my mother asked for a sharp knife and proceeded to cut the walking stick into small pieces which she gave us to chew. I looked on my share of this delicacy with a certain amount of distrust and nibbled at it doubtfully; but as it turned out to be sweet and my sisters seemed to be enjoying it, I did as they did and thus had my first taste of sugar cane, America's first token, to me, of her existence.

The school I attended was a little house at the bottom of a very long garden, at about ten minutes' walk from our house. Lina took me there every morning. She was a peasant girl from a place in Dordogne called Badefol d'Anse (how could one ever forget such a name?) and I liked her well enough, although she threw my shoes at my head in the morning, by way of telling me that it was time to get started. My sisters, who suffered the same treatment at her hands, resented these rustic manners and complained clamorously to my mother. I simply dodged the shoes and said

14

nothing, because in other ways Lina was extremely nice to me. For instance, she would allow me to steal into the kitchen after meals and help her wash the dishes. Then she would dance the *bourrée* for me, as they danced it in her village, to the accompaniment of a song which, I feel sure, must have gone back to the days before Caesar conquered the Gauls.

When I remember what she looked like, I do not wonder that I was amused by her dancing. She was a red-cheeked person with an impertinent nose, a large bust, and heavy hips encased in a tight-fitting black dress. Even to see her walk was something of a treat. She wore long pointed black shoes and moved forward, toes well out, chin high, with a look of defiance. Once a month, her brother came to see her. He was a butler in my godmother's service and did not strike me as being as picturesque as Lina. He was loutish enough, however, and I remember this about him: he always went downstairs with his back turned the wrong way, as if the staircase had been a ladder.

Having been walked to school by Lina, I was at that point placed in the hands of a mild-eyed lady called Mademoiselle Marie, who tried to teach me how to read, by no means an easy job. I was slow and never listened, because I was homesick for the rue de Passy. Finally, I and the silliest of the children in the lower form were taught to do a sort of simplified tatting, with an old spool of thread, a ball of bright colored wool and an ordinary pin; yards and yards of this gay looking stuff came out of the spool as we sang:

Il court, il court, le furet . . .

an old Canadian song about a ferret running through the woods.

This was about all Mademoiselle Marie ever taught me; I am quite sure that I could not tell A from B when I left her school. Yet I cannot look back on those days without a feeling of regret, almost of longing, because I now realize that I was then as happy as a small boy can be, and whatever happiness I may have experienced in later years could never be quite the same kind of emotion, with its utter lack of self-consciousness. Above all, I could never again feel happy for the *first time:* happiness would become more and more something I would crave because I had tasted of it and wanted more; the element of surprise was taken away from it forever. I could no longer stand like a tiny Faustus in a black apron and all of a sudden discover that the old world I happened to be in was a place of inexpressible beauty, that the clouds above my head were as lovely as anything I could see, and that the cool air of an October morning filled one's heart with a desire to live forever. I remember standing alone in the school garden and listening to someone beating a rug in the neighborhood. This
16

memory is prosaic enough, and why it should have floated up after so many years, when so much else is forgotten, I cannot say, except that from another direction came the sound of a distant piano playing Mozart's "Turkish March," a piece with which I was very familiar because my sister Mary played it at home. It must have been a few minutes before eight o'clock, on a fall morning in 1905; I felt so unaccountably elated that I have never quite lost the memory of that feeling, which has lingered within me through the darkest times. The first cool days after summer never come around without bringing at least a hint of that early happiness.

What has always struck me about childhood is it's secrecy. A child seldom expresses what he feels otherwise than by singing when he is happy or screaming when he is afraid, his subtler emotions remaining necessarily wrapped in silence because he has no words at his command to convey his meaning. True, he talks to himself, as I did, in a low mumbling voice. I had invented a language by means of which I had taken myself into my own confidence. This secret language was rich and varied. How simple it was to master will be realized when I disclose the fact that it was merely an imitation of what my elders' conversation sounded like to my ear. No words were clearly recognizable, but, in this stream of half formed vowels and consonants, joy, sorrow, amusement, surprise and sometimes fierce anger

sary to slap us; like the angel in Baudelaire's poem, she chastised us, but not in wrath. To use a popular French phrase, she was outwardly as stiff as the law — *"raide comme la justice"* — but I suspect that she hid a tender heart in her capacious bosom, and also that she wrote poetry. This, however, is entirely beside the question.

"Forty little French monkeys," was my mother's description of the boys in my class, "and Julian", she added, "looks exactly like one too." This, to her, was at once a cause for amusement and vexation. She loved the French almost as much as she loved her own people, but she wanted me to be American. She wanted all her children to be American and loathed the thought that some of us had a decided French accent in English. Her task was a difficult one, but she was determined to succeed.

Every day, she read the Bible to us in the Authorized Version. I remember that even when I was too small to follow what she read, I used to sit at her feet and listen to her voice. I liked the sound of the English Bible, although it remained incomprehensible to me. One day, however, something new and exciting happened: my mother read a verse and I understood it, I understood it from beginning to end; it made sense. I tried to say something, but my mother told me to be quiet and went on with her reading. Since then, I have often made vigorous efforts to recall the first sentence out of the Bible which I was able to understand, but all in vain. Yet I still hope that, as I grow older and my memory goes back further, I shall find it gleaming in the dark.

When I was about seven, this same Bible was placed in my hands and I was made to learn "Blessed is the man," "The Lord is my shepherd," and "Why do the heathen rage?" Indeed, why the heathen raged was a complete mystery to me, but I was quite pleased to hear that they were going to be dashed in pieces like a potter's vessel and I stamped my foot as I recited these angry verses to myself. Before leaving the subject, I cannot help mentioning that my mother's Bible was filled with marginal inscriptions which puzzled me as much as anything in the book itself. She had been given this Bible as a girl and marked a considerable number of verses with a cross, adding remarks of this type: "Never forget the morning of July 17, 1886." Or "Remember October 12, 1875." One or two dates would certainly have had something very touching about them, but there were so many that even she had to laugh. My elder sisters pestered her for details: "Mamma, what *did* happen on the morning of July 17, 1886? Did someone propose to you?" "No, you silly girl." "Well, do try to remember." "I can't." "Well then, tell us what happened on the evening of March 19, 1891." "Go away, miss. I am not going to be cross-questioned. Leave me alone and learn your psalms."

So deeply impressed was I with the Bible and particularly with the Old Testament, that my mother gave me an illustrated book of Scripture stories which I eagerly read, poring over the pictures until every detail found its place in my memory. Soon after this I conceived the idea of becoming a high-priest and offering up a burnt sacrifice. The staggering difficulties of such a plan did not discourage me in the least. The first thing, I thought, was to dress as nearly as possible like the high-priest in my book. A Turkish towel around my head and my mother's red dressing gown looped up with safety pins gave what I considered the desire effect. Next, a high altar had to be produced. There was no high altar in the house, but our sewing machine did well enough as a substitute provided the hood was placed on it, and it was. Another Turkish towel was then fetched and spread on the altar to make it look exactly like the picture. I got two candlesticks from the kitchen and stood them at either end of the altar with my father's hair brushes between them to take the place of the "shew bread."

At this point, I was beset with fresh difficulties. To begin with, as my picture book clearly proved, the shew bread did not belong on the high altar, but I explained to the crowd of at least threescore and ten thousand Jews who were attending this ceremony, that we were one altar short and that this one would have to do. Everybody agreed that it was all right and I now wondered what I was going to offer up. A calf or a bullock was out of the question, but an article of value and splendor might perhaps prove acceptable to the Almighty. The thought of sacrificing one of my toys flashed through my mind, but somehow none of them seemed worthy of such an honor. After looking about in the room for a while and finding nothing, I walked into the hall and beheld my father's top hat on the wall.

Now this hat was made of silk and had a glistening brightness about it which I thought lovely, an opinion which I shared with my mother, who used a small brown velvet cushion to wipe the dust off this precious object. And there they both hung on the rack, the top hat and the little brown velvet cushion. I looked at the hat with a mixture of awe and envy, and all of a sudden a bold thought made its way into my brain: I would offer up my father's top hat.

It was easy enough to reach by climbing on a chair, and I bore it triumphantly to the high altar where I placed it with marks of profound respect between the two candlesticks. The next question to solve was whether I should offer it up in a symbolical sort of way or actually set fire to it, which, of course, would be more in keeping with Old Testament tradition. On the other hand, something told me that it was both naughty and dangerous to burn

23

my father's silk hat. Yet the urge to do so must have been almost irresistible, for I ran to the kitchen for matches.

Fortunately my mother's attention had been aroused by my running about, and curiosity drew her to the room where the holocaust was to take place. By that time I had come back with a box of matches which I had stolen in the cook's absence, and I suppose that I looked terribly guilty; my mouth was open, I had no explanation to offer. With a swift gesture, my mother rescued the hat and took it back to its abiding place in the hall, I running after her in her own dressing gown and screaming that it was all a burnt sacrifice. But I was completely misunderstood and the experiment a disastrous failure: the high-priest was turned over on his mother's knee and spanked.

The hat, however, was not saved for a very long time. Like many lovely things in this world, it was doomed, as we shall see.

CHAPTER THREE

In 1907, my cousin Sarah Elliott came from America to spend the summer with us and stayed until the World War was over. That is what Paris does to American girls. She wore sailor hats, a large black bow at the back of her head, and played "The Merry Widow" on our piano in a halting sort of way but with great energy. I suppose that I seemed as strange to her as she did to me, and we both thought of each other as intensely foreign. She was about sixteen, with light blue eyes, freckles on her nose and beautiful, untidy auburn hair.

Being then a little over six, it was difficult for me to make her out. On the one hand, she spoke much like my father and mother and frequently mentioned her home-town, Savannah, in the existence of which I had at last come to believe. I realized, however, that she did not say the things that my parents said about America. She referred to buildings they had not seen and, in the same way, they alluded to homes and people she knew nothing of, to such an extent that I sometimes wondered if they were talking about the same place. Nevertheless, they seemed to agree that my grandfather's house stood on Madison Square, and that Bull and Broad were parallel.

There were far more subtle differences which escaped me altogether, although my sisters were probably aware of them. The songs Sarah knew and even attempted to sing were unknown to us; her phrases were not ours, her slang seemed as obscure as a foreign language. This was all plain enough, but there was something else: there was the war.

Our point of view was that of our parents who had taught us to think of the Southern flag as our flag, as indeed it was. However, they had left the States some twenty years earlier, bringing with them ideas of their time which were not subjected to alterations in France, but might have undergone important changes had my parents remained in America. This brings us to a very interesting point upon which I wish I could dwell, because its historical significance is very great, as I have recently had occasion to ascertain.

Danton once said that you do not take away your country's soil on the soles of your feet, meaning, I suppose, that when a man leaves his country, he leaves behind him whatever makes him a Frenchman, or a German, or an American. I wonder how true this is, and how false. What a man takes away with him is his country at a given moment of its history; but the country he has left goes on developing and changing, whereas the country he has taken with him and carries, so to speak, in his breast remains what it was, sacred but somewhat stunted. If the expatriate's vitality, imagination and strength of resistance are strong, however, his country, which has become a sort of inner fatherland, develops on lines of its own. That is what happened to American colonists and that, in a minor way, is what happened to my parents. Their America was intensely real, but necessarily old-fashioned. One of the greatest surprises I had when I first came to this country was the realization that people of my generation were not so interested in the Civil War as I was, and that they really knew and cared little about it. To me, the Civil War was a cause of great sadness, because I had not lived in the country where it had taken place and where the feeling about the tragic differences between North and South had to a great extent disappeared. To me, indeed, the war had just been fought and we had just lost it, or so it seemed from my mother's account. In a way, we were brought up in a small post-bellum America and in a reconstruction atmosphere.

A first hint of this was given to us when my cousin Sarah came over. She was, of course, a loyal Southerner, but she lacked a little of our grim earnestness. There was something of a commotion, one day, when she began picking out "Marching through Georgia" on our piano. My mother, whose ear was not particularly musical, nevertheless recognized the hated tune and flew out of her bedroom looking more like a personification of a storm than a human being. A brief altercation followed and tears were shed; and that was the last time Sherman's boys marched through our house.

I remember feeling so upset about our defeat that I dreaded the times when my mother used to tell us about it. We had had such magnificent victories early in the war, that in some unaccountable way I always hoped we would win, in spite of the fact that I knew we had lost. I felt like the lady who, being told of some particularly distressing and well-known episode in the Bible, was heard to exclaim: "Dear, dear, let's hope it isn't true!"

At school, being then in my eighth year, I began reading French history and was taught first of all about "our ancestors the Gauls" with their blue eyes, long hair and their apparently unceasing fear that the sky might tumble down on them during storms. It was strange, but I liked thinking of the Gauls as my ancestors too, although I had been told by my mother that we did not have a drop of French blood in our veins. In spite of anything she could say, I became French the moment I crossed the threshold of our classroom and put on my black alpaca apron.

Memories of Happy Days

There I sat with thirty-five or forty boys of my age, scribbling in a copybook with tongue well out or watching Monsieur Lesellier gesticulate in front of the blackboard. He was a tall man with a goat-like face and a gray beard which he pulled at in the approved fashion. His hair was cut short and brushed back; his blue eyes twinkled ironically behind a small pince-nez perched on top of a long reddish nose. Everything about him seemed impressive: his height, his shuffling gait and above all the long black coat under the tails of which he hid his hands and made his knuckles crack. His talk was liberally sprinkled with the salt of atticism and his asides were lost on us, but I recognized some of his quiet little jokes, in later years, when I read Anatole France.

I admired Monsieur Lesellier. I admired him to such a point that I thought nothing more desirable than to be exactly like him, a brilliant man with a beautiful pince-nez and a frock coat down to one's knees, and of course I insisted on having the same ancestors, viz. the Gauls. One day, without wanting to, I suppose, he dealt me a cruel blow by asking me if my parents were English. I said they were American. "Any wild Indians in your family, *mon petit ami*?" I was bewildered, I said I didn't know. I didn't care for Indians, I preferred Gauls with long red moustaches like our baker's and steel helmets. "But," rejoined Monsieur Lesellier, "if you are American, there may be an Indian or two among your forefathers, but no Gauls. Now don't look so disturbed," he said pushing me back gently to my seat, "I'll teach you and your comrades a Gallic war-song."

He then took a tuning fork out of a drawer and, having adjusted his voice to the right tone, proceeded to sing a terrifying ballad about dead men's blood being drunk out of their skulls by their enemies, after the battle, and about riding through the storm on white mares and cutting off one's enemy's head with a sword. After many years, I can still hear the wild refrain sung in a quavering voice:

> *Tam, tam, tirelo,*
> *Bois le sang des morts, ma chèvre!*

Monsieur Lesellier regretted that the accompaniment could not be that of a sword striking a buckler, as it should have been; nevertheless, we were enchanted with his rendition of this savage piece of music, which we speedily mastered.

I was particularly delighted with Monsieur Lesellier's war song and ran home with great hopes of impressing and, if possible, frightening my mother by stamping my foot and singing *Tam, tam, tirelo,* but my performance only puzzled her.

"Who does he think he is now?" she asked my eldest

sister. "Last week, we had a high-priest on our hands. To-day, this. Ask the little French monkey what he means, Eleanor."

My sister asked me in French.

"I am a Gaul," said I fiercely.

"You are just a plain American," said my mother. "Who ever heard of a child of mine calling himself a Gaul? *Gaulois* indeed!"

This was disappointing, and I asked if my ancestors were Indians.

"Indians? No. Certainly not. Your ancestors were English."

"And Scotch," added my sister.

My mother agreed.

"Cattle-thieves," Eleanor went on as she polished her nails. "They lived on the Lowlands border and stole cattle from the English."

She seemed quite proud of our robber ancestors and would gladly have given me more information about them, had not my mother changed the subject. I felt terribly frustrated. The idea of having thieves as ancestors was not a pleasant one. Thieves in one's family are difficult to explain to strangers. Warriors sound better, and I wanted to tell my schoolmates that we too had warriors among our forefathers, like the French. These thoughts were too plainly written in my looks for my mother not to read them. She therefore proceeded to tell me about the first inhabitants of Britain, and I listened carefully. On the following day, I informed my friends at school that our ancestors were called Picts, but no one seemed ever to have heard of the Picts, and when I said that their national trait was to paint their bodies black and blue, it was plain to see that my audience considered this pointless, barbarous and disgusting.

CHAPTER FOUR

Unless it was really cold, the windows in the house were left open, and it was one of our favorite forms of entertainment to sit by them and watch the people in the rue de Passy. I don't suppose that any street in the whole world will ever seem as beautiful to me as the rue de Passy when I was six. It was noisy and I love quiet, but I think that if I could once more hear the sound of horses' hoofs on the wooden pavement or the clatter of the old-fashioned double-decked tram on its way to the Hôtel de Ville, I should welcome the noise with gratitude. Early in the morning, when the maid opened the drawing-room window, it seemed to me that the whole street came into the room with its cabs, its buses and its busy crowd composed mainly of servants with baskets over their arms. Occasionally, a butcher boy would go by on his bicycle, whistling tunes which no Frenchman could listen to now without a pang, if he were old enough to remember those days.

It is sad to reflect that the noise of city streets, annoying as it may be to some, dies down in time and stops forever, leaving no memory in anyone's mind. We can only very vaguely imagine what the main street of Athens sounded like under the government of Pericles, or the Forum when Tiberius reigned, or the Place de Grève in medieval Paris. Sometimes, a song brings us an echo of what was heard, a few lines by Villon or some street cry which has been preserved by tradition, and that is all. I hope the means at our disposal in the present time will inspire someone with the desire to record the voice of Times Square or Piccadilly Circus, in order that future generations may form a distinct idea of what we heard in our day.

What I shall never forget is the tremendous volume of sound created by my mother's favorite bus, the much lamented Passy-Bourse. This huge vehicle was painted a canary yellow, perched on very large wheels and drawn by two heavy Percheron horses. In bad weather, it was better to sit inside the coach, but on a fine summer afternoon nothing was more exciting, I thought, than climbing up the narrow stairway at my mother's heels and sitting by her on what was called the *impériale*. The *impériale* was open to the sky and in no way protected against the sun or rain, but it seems to me that it was always crowded. Perhaps it was cheaper. With luck, a small boy could find room just back of the coachman, a much coveted seat which I struggled hard to obtain. It was fun to hear the long whip

34

crack above one's head with a noise like a pistol shot, and to watch the dappled rumps of the horses move up and down as those mighty animals trotted along the rue de Passy. Also, it gave one a feeling of importance to be seated so near the coachman. He wore a dark blue coat and a shiny black hat with a low crown and a broadish brim. Most of the coachmen employed by the *Compagnie des Omnibus* were heavy fellows with red faces and one of them, I remember, added to the beauty of his appearance by wearing large rings in his ears, but it must be understood that this was a personal touch. My mother was of the opinion that these earrings were brass; I preferred to believe that they were made of gold. Be that as it may, the driver of the Passy-Bourse considered himself the lord and master of every street he took us through. Everything and everybody gave way in front of him. Now that I look back on those delightful rides, it seems to me that we charged rather than drove. That is what made things so exciting. People scattered in all directions when we came rumbling on and I felt certain that we would sooner or later upset a vendor's cart or go crashing into a cab. More than once I shut my eyes tight in order not to see the horrible sight which I expected, but nothing ever happened. What surprised me more than anything else was that the enormous vehicle never turned over when it left the rue de Passy to plunge into the narrow rue Guichard. This street was indeed so narrow and the bus so large that I always wondered how one could contain the other. As the rue Guichard happened to be paved with cobble stones and was, for some reason, always taken at a gallop, the bus shook so violently that the windowpanes vibrated and my fat cheeks trembled like jelly.

So down the rue Guichard, up the rue de la Pompe to the avenue Victor Hugo, and up the avenue Victor Hugo to the Place de l'Etoile and its wide expanse. Then on again, thundering down the avenue de Friedland, where we stopped a few minutes at the top of the rue du Faubourg Saint Honoré, just long enough to add an extra horse to our fuming team. . . .

Those happy days can never return. The Passy-Bourse was one of the last remnants of the nineteenth century and with it went a great many of the more amiable aspects of life. It disappeared shortly before the war of 1914. Some years ago, an unfortunate attempt was made to revive it for a few hours, for one brief afternoon in April. Once more, the old yellow coach was seen careering down the boulevard de la Madeleine, but somehow it didn't look the same; it looked small and funny, and people laughed at it. I did not care for this: it was as if a part of my childhood had been held up to ridicule, and I sadly turned away, pretending not to see.

Memories of Happy Days.

Once in a while, my mother took me to see her best
friend, Agnes Farley, who lived in a dark flat in the rue
de la Paix. We would stumble up a black staircase and be
shown into a drawing room which smelled of cigar smoke.
There was a bust of Caesar on the mantelpiece and a crystal chandelier hung from the middle of the ceiling, and
every time a bus went by, the chandelier would jingle
faintly. About five or six gilt armchairs were arranged in
a wide semi-circle and gleamed in the afternoon sun. I tried
to sit in each of them before Agnes appeared; if I succeeded
in doing so, I considered it an excellent sign. I should have
been at a loss to explain what this sign portended, but I
cherished this superstition as something of my own.

Agnes would march in, preceded by a yapping dog. She
was a stout woman with an ugly face and a charming smile.
A small cigar was perpetually burning between her fingers.
Her clothes, her books, her dog, everything about her was
strongly scented with those cigars known, I believe, as
niñas. She was Irish but had lived in France most of her
life and spoke French with only a trace of her native accent, which was rather pleasing to a Latin ear. Her laughter covered the roar of the street below her windows and
although I could not understand anything she said, I
laughed as often as she did. There was something almost
intoxicating in her mirth. Nothing she said or did seemed
exactly like what other people said or did; she knew how

37

to make trite things appear unusual and interesting, which is really the essence of talent. One was amazed at the unexpected beauty of the world as long as she was there to point it out; no sooner had one left her than people seemed dull once more and the very light seemed to fade.

She never spoke to me otherwise than to a grownup. That was one of my reasons for liking her. It is flattering to be addressed as a man when one is hardly ten. "And what do *you* think of the railroad strike?" she would ask me. "Do you consider it right of Briand to bring out the troops? No, of course you don't. You are a sensible Frenchman with liberal ideas." I gaped and grinned. At other times, we discussed literature. "So they are making you read *Le Cid.* Well, that is what comes of being born in France, my dear. A more tiresome story than *Le Cid,* I can't imagine can you?" I couldn't. ". . . or more unnatural, more inhuman. Absurd ideas expressed in stilted lines. . ." I agreed. "Let me ask you as a sensible Frenchman if you make such an awful row about your daughter's love affairs? No, I thought not. My dear, you and I had better stick to our old favorites, the *Tempest* and *Tristram Shandy.* Have you read Anatole France's latest book? No? Mary, your son is awfully *blasé* if he can't read France. Well, try *Le Livre de mon Ami* all the same, my friend. You will appreciate the style even if you do find his point of view old-fashioned. . . ."

38

And so forth. I sat entranced and mystified, with a bun in my hand and an admiring look in my eye. It was delightful not to be ordered to go and play by a dignified grownup, but to be requested to join the conversation, in spite of the fact that, like most children, I must have been what Agnes called "a bit of a bore."

She was passionately fond of English and French literature and lazily wrote two charming books on the French countryside. Most of her time was spent in her little parlor where she smoked cigars and read. Once a day, towards the end of the afternoon, she would take a very short walk from her flat to the Place Vendôme, about two hundred yards away, or to the Place de l'Opéra, where she sat at the Café de la Paix and watched the people go by. I have often lamented her death, which occurred when I was twelve and she a little over forty. Had she lived long enough for me to appreciate her great good sense and exquisite humor, I might have profited by her advice and avoided many literary mistakes.

From time to time, she took my mother to task on the way I spoke English. "You know, my dear, it is all right for him to be a sensible Frenchman, but he drops his aitches. You can't allow your son to grow up and drop his aitches like Bennett." But it wasn't my mother's fault. To hear me recite the Psalms with a French accent was a source of great mortification to her, and no amount of correcting

39

seemed to improve my speech. This was all the stranger
since my sisters, with one exception, spoke their mother
tongue admirably.

Mine was a peculiar case. Although we had repeatedly
been told that our flag was the Southern flag, a small
water color of which hung in our parlor, this in no way
interfered with the fact that when Monsieur Mougeot
told us about the horrors of 1870 and the humiliation of
Sedan, I invariably cried.

Today, it strikes me as an astounding absurdity that a
child of eight or ten should be made miserable by the
thought of military defeats which occurred forty years before he was born, but I suppose that this is a part of what
we are pleased to call education. Eighteen seventy was referred to as *l'Année terrible* and seldom mentioned without moans and sighs. Our professors, some of whom were
old enough to have fought against the Germans, instilled
in us the proper feeling of resentment and the hope that
some day Alsace-Lorraine would return to France.

There must have been some kind of magic in the name
of Alsace-Lorraine, for however turbulent and undisci-
plined he might have been at other times, a French child
always looked up with a serious and attentive air whenever the lost provinces were mentioned. A peculiar sadness
seemed to be connected with the war, a sadness best sym-

bolized by the huge black bow worn by the women in certain sections of Alsace. France, it was felt, was in mourning for her child, but except in some of Déroulède's doggerel songs, no yearning for revenge was expressed.

Since I have mentioned the name of Déroulède, I cannot help saying a few words about him, because he is linked with so many memories of our childhood. Whether he was a great man or not is, thank goodness, not for me to decide. He was a good Frenchman and a bad poet, a bad poet whom thousands of Frenchmen considered no less than inspired, Déroulède himself being the most firmly convinced of this highly questionable fact.

He wore a white goatee, a wide brimmed hat and a black Lavallière, like a poet in mourning, and never appeared in public except in a long frock coat which was cut in a somewhat military style. Once a year, he would head a delegation from a patriotic society and march to the Strasbourg statue, on the Place de la Concorde, bearing a wreath in his hand and some fresh piece of doggerel in his mind. In a most amusing book called *1900*, Paul Morand has given us a lively picture of this annual ceremony. I cannot remember the exact words he uses to describe Déroulède, but I do recall that when the patriot scales the high pedestal to place his wreath at the foot of the statue, Morand wittily compares him to a goat climbing on its favorite rock.

41

Today, in the face of the most shocking catastrophe in French History, it is no longer possible to laugh at the old gentleman who had so much of the real French spirit in him, but before the war of 1914 it was not infrequent to hear people make fun of him and his jingo verses. No one seriously entertained the thought of revenge, and although there was little love lost between the French and the Germans, I cannot say that we children were ever taught to hate the people on the other side of the Rhine; but we were told, wisely, I believe, not to trust them.

Of course, there were fire-eaters like honest Monsieur Mougeot who could not mention Bismark without growling out the name and pounding his desk for sheer rage, but as a rule, sentiments of this kind were not given vent to. Our professor of German was an Alsatian by the name of Kessler, an ex-cavalry officer who wore a tight-waisted frock coat and a most impressive monocle on a long black ribbon. He was youngish, though bald-headed, and never allowed himself to hurl insults at the German government but wielded sarcasm with incomparable grace and the ease of a fencing master. German thickheadedness was the butt of most of his jokes and he would make our classroom ring with the sound of laughter at the expense of what we then called the Prussians.

At home, my sisters and I were given supplementary lessons in German by a lady from Munich whose name was

Fräulein Margreiter. One of our chief amusements was to ask her where she came from (pretending that we had forgotten), because of the funny way in which she wrinkled up her nose when she said Muenchen. A quiet, modest person usually dressed in brown, with a rabbit-like profile and untidy black hair which fell over her eyes, she was obsequiously polite and caused much embarrassment to my mother by kissing her hand. We liked her well enough although she was something of a bore, but now I come to think of it she could not be held responsible for the wildly irregular verbs of the German tongue. She always addressed us in a serious, low-toned voice and used the longest French words she could think of, when she spoke in that language. Her nervous shyness and anxious look spoke of a thwarted life, while her old brown dress came to be in my mind a symbol of poverty and sadness. When the war broke out, she disappeared.

When I look back on those days and see how modern children behave, I realize that boys and girls of 1940 would have found us easily amused and possibly a little foolish. Somehow we managed to be happy without radios and moving pictures. We played hide and seek and musical chairs, bartered stamps and fought over Japanese puzzles. My sister Retta, who was then about twelve, would sometimes sit on the floor by the window and count all the vehicles that went by, making notes in a tiny hand on the first page of a large copy-book which she had bought for that purpose and intended to fill. But she never went further than the first page, finding, I suppose, that after the first hour or so it became a little tedious to add up trams, buses, cabs, vans and carts. However, I wish we had kept this tentative description of the rue de Passy traffic. To me, it would be a matter of great interest to learn, for instance, that on the 23rd of April 1908, fifteen cabs trotted up or down our old street between the hours of two

44

and three P.M. I should enjoy thinking on what business they went about, what frivolous couples they were taking to the Bois or what sour-faced attorneys to gloomy offices near the Madeleine.

Retta was a silent and reflective child with a serious and beautiful face, unfathomable black eyes and heavy black hair which covered her shoulders. We none of us felt that we knew her well, because she was sparing of words and never imparted a secret to anyone, but she was so lovely to behold and so sweet-tempered that she always had plenty of friends. What was strangest about her was a rather sinister sense of humor, but I shall come to that later.

As I grew a little older, my own amusements took on a literary turn and I liked to believe that I should some day be a great actor like the actor who played the part of Mr. Fogg in *Around the World in Eighty Days*. With that purpose in mind, I began learning lines from famous dramas, by way of being good and ready when I should be called upon to appear on the stage. The fact that I did not understand half of what I recited did not seem to matter much in my eyes. What I wanted was to stamp about in my room and use big words, and imagine that I was not myself but some important and clever person like Augustus or Cyrano de Bergerac.

Thursday was the day I most looked forward to, because

45

it was a holiday and also because our sempstress, Mademoiselle Félicité Goudeau, came to sew early in the morning and stayed until supper time. She was my audience. All things considered, her part was easy enough as it consisted merely in quietly doing her work while I shouted at her. At times, I might shake my fist in her face or wave a dagger over her head, but there had been an understanding beforehand that all this was drama, and she took it well enough.

She was a shy little creature with frizzly gray hair and a short, quick step which took her in and out of rooms so swiftly that one was inevitably reminded of a mouse or of any such furtive animal. As a rule, she wore a black apron and went about with pins between her teeth. This disturbed me a little, as I preferred her to be seated and not move. I told her so, one day, and a long argument took place, ending with my mother being called in to arbitrate. Of course, I was ordered out of the room but came back later "breathing out threatenings and slaughter" in the approved manner of the *Comédie Française*.

We called her Goudeau for short. When she happened to be in a good mood, my ranting amused her and she would laugh quietly to herself, shaking her gray head, but there was a certain testiness about her which my mother ascribed to some disappointing love affair in earlier life. "She must have been right pretty. I can see traces of good

46

looks in her face." It was one of my mother's traits to see vestiges of beauty in people's wrinkles as well as hidden kindness in their souls, but my sisters protested: "Goudeau! She is almost humpbacked and has a pointed red nose!" "She wasn't born with a red nose, you silly girls, and she is not humpbacked, she is simply a little round-shouldered from overwork."

I certainly did not think Goudeau attractive, but she was indispensable. One day I flew at her and roared: "You have dishonored my daughter! Out with your rapier, devil, and defend yourself!" She giggled softly and straightened her iron rimmed pince-nez. "Don't deny it!" I went on fiercely, "my daughter will testify against you herself."

With these words I ran to the kitchen, opened the cupboard under Lina's astonished eyes, and seizing one of those heavy four pound loaves of bread which were then sold, wrapped a napkin around it. The next thing I needed was a dagger, but daggers were scarce in the house, so I took the bread-knife instead and hurried back to the room.

"Here is my daughter," I bellowed. "She has come to accuse you publicly."

"Your daughter must be awfully young if she has to be carried about in swaddling clothes," remarked Goudeau with a sarcastic cackle. "Are you sure that she is the right one, Monsieur Julien?"

I ordered the hell-fiend to be silent and, deciding that

47

I had rather see my daughter dead than dishonored, I stabbed her, sending the bread-knife repeatedly through the loaf.

"Now," said Goudeau, "she is both dead *and* dishonored. What are you going to do?"

"Kill you!" was the answer.

Whereupon Goudeau rose from her work and ran for my mother. I was forbidden to do *Le Roi s'amuse* any more and the bread was taken away from me by an indignant cook.

Surprisingly enough, this kind of thing went on for years. For years, Goudeau came to sew on Thursdays, growing whiter and whiter with age and more and more bent, and for years I threatened the old demoiselle with immediate destruction if she did not give me the names of her accomplices, or surrender the keys of the city, or divulge the place where that bag of gold doubloons lay concealed. She went on sewing patiently, and I believe that in time she came to like me in spite of my noisy affiliations with Victor Hugo and Pierre Corneille.

Some weeks after the incident of the dishonored bread loaf, Goudeau came to my mother and explained that she could no longer work without a dummy. She explained that she had to have a dummy on a stand, like all other sempstresses, and my father, who was consulted on the subject, decided that by all means she must have one. This

48

turned out to be a mistake, although at first blush it seemed a reasonable plan.

Ten days or so elapsed and the dummy was brought to the house. I did not think it a very interesting object, at first, but Goudeau seemed enchanted with it and felt its hips with an approving hand. As far as dummies go, I suppose that it was a particularly fine specimen. The chest came out in aggressive lines which were set off by lovely curves at the back, the whole affair being black and shiny, supported by what looked like a broomstick. When a dress was put on the dummy, one got the impression of a smart and rather fussy lady whose head and arms had been chopped off without her minding it much, because she looked quite natural without them, but when Goudeau took off the dress, there was something positively embarrassing about the dummy's sable nakedness.

Little by little, I came to look on it with different eyes. Even undressed, it had a tremendous dignity of bearing. I called it Coucou Blanc after a character in Daudet's *Petit Chose,* and it seemed to me that by giving the dummy a name I gave it a soul and made a heart beat in its magnificent breast. Coucou Blanc, then, became a real person. She was so tall that Goudeau had to get up on a chair to reach her shoulders. It was not long before I instinctively turned towards her when I addressed Hector's widow, the inconsolable Andromache, or Queen Athaliah whom the dogs devoured. Her *hauteur* was impressive and somehow suggested tragedy.

For some time, I did not dare touch her, but I suppose that seeing Goudeau mercilessly stick pins into her altered my attitude towards Coucou Blanc. When the sempstress wanted to move her from one corner of the room to the other, she would make her topple over and catch her in her little arms, then drag her to the place she thought best. There was something so ignominious about this treatment that I lost all respect for the dark lady and one day, having read about Rebecca and Front-de-Boeuf, in *Ivanhoe,* I suddenly pounced on Coucou Blanc and abducted her from the room. She was much lighter than might have been expected and we careered triumphantly through the apartment, followed by an irate and protesting Goudeau who tried to rescue her child and only succeeded in precipitating the very accident which she dreaded: as I was running with my prey — who was about twice as tall as I was — I fell headlong in a narrow passage and sent Coucou Blanc hurtling above me. There was a crash, and the shaft of the dummy snapped in two as if it had been glass.

My mother immediately appeared on the scene like a Nemesis. What followed was so commonplace as not to deserve any mention, save that it was painful. Crippled Coucou Blanc was restored to her former position in my parents' bedroom, but being much diminished in size, she had to be placed on a low table where she no longer looked like a princess from the land of Cush or the widowed queen of the Trojan hero, but rather like some horrible remains pulled out of a burning house.

Once a year, on Saint Charlemagne's day — which falls
sometime in January — the boys from the upper forms at
Janson, my school, made a point of marching to the rue du
Ranelagh and invading the Lycée Molière, one of the city's
largest girls' schools, which my sisters attended. Why
Saint Charlemagne's day should have been chosen for this
expedition, I could never find out. It will be remembered
that the holy emperor, with the help of the English monk
Alcwin, founded the first schools in what was later to be
called France. However, I can see no connection between
this fact and the sudden appearance of an evil-looking goat
in the head-mistress's office, nor was it ever clearly explained how the boys managed to get the animal past the
front door where two policemen were supposed to keep
watch. Nevertheless, it is recorded in the archives of the
Préfecture de Police that the outrage I have described was
committed on a winter afternoon, in 1908 or 1909, by a
band of rowdy students who defied the headmistress and
jeered at her, causing much confusion among the faculty

and, I suppose, considerable amusement among the girls, which may have been the end in view.

My sister Anne gave a full and excited account of that eventful day to her mother, who laughed heartily over it. Retta, my youngest sister after Lucy, was far more reticent on the subject, although she had seen as much as Anne. It was remarkable how little she spoke. She played and seemed to enjoy herself as much as anyone, but whatever went on in her head she kept to herself. Her love of books, the care with which she wrote her *devoirs,* and above all her serious, attentive look singled her out in the eyes of her teachers as one of their most interesting pupils; she was that, to be sure, but not in the way those good people imagined.

For some reason which she never divulged, she took it into her head to play a joke on three or four of the ladies in charge of the school. They did not know it, neither did anyone else; indeed, not a soul suspected what thoughts were being entertained by this quiet little girl in her neat black apron, whom her teachers patted on the head for being such a *bonne élève.* She came home every afternoon at half past four, ate her bread and chocolate like every child in France, then arranged her copy-books and dictionaries on the dining-room table and wrote out her task in that flawless hand of hers which made each page a masterpiece of penmanship.

We all worked at the dining-room table, under the wheezy gas chandelier, fighting over the atlas, upsetting the ink on the green baize cover. Only Retta was really good, and quiet. When her work was done, she would get her stamp album out of a drawer and lovingly examine the dirty little pieces of colored paper which she prized above all her possessions. Or she would bring out her work basket and embroider a handkerchief. We all loved her, even though she was perpetually being held up to us as an example.

One day, my mother came home with the unbelievable news that Retta had been expelled from the Lycée Molière. No one scolded the child, not a word was said about what she had done, and she was simply sent to another school kept by some English ladies. My parents did not seem at all perturbed about all this; they even showed signs of amusement, but it was only a long time after that I learned what had happened.

Her plan had been carefully thought out. She first obtained her victims' private addresses, then went to two or three of the largest stores in the city and asked for their catalogues which were given to her as a matter of course. Having taken home this literature, she perused it secretly and pondered a long time before making up her lists and writing the necessary letters.

Some time elapsed; then one morning, the ladies whom

54

Retta had picked out were called to their respective back
doors by employees from the *Bon Marché*, the *Galeries
Lafayette* and, I believe, *Dufayel*. The staircases were filled
with men groaning under the weight of steamer trunks,
bathtubs, wardrobes, kitchen tables, sofas, beds. The ladies
looked and did not understand. By way of explanation,
they were handed bills which they indignantly handed
back. Meanwhile, the streets were thrown into a state of
excitement by the presence of large delivery vans out
of which the most heterogeneous objects were being
taken and slowly carried into the houses: bird cages and
rabbit coops, bookcases, perambulators (this was a naughty
touch because Retta knew very well that her victims were
maiden ladies); last and more baffling than all the
rest, a handsome casket had grimly been added for full
measure.

Needless to say, the teachers were beside themselves
with surprise and anger. To telephone to the stores was out
of the question — they had no such luxury as a telephone;
on the other hand, the delivery men refused to believe that
there could be any mistake. Indeed they had been given
the right names and the right addresses, but the argument
did not center on that point: what was contended on one
side and frenziedly denied on the other was that the para-
phernalia had been ordered by the persons whose names
were written on the bills. Finally, everything was taken

55

downstairs and put back into the vans in the presence of hilarious crowds.

When the victims appeared in their classrooms that morning (all had been nicely timed so that they would be good and late and, it was hoped, would incur Madame la Directrice's much dreaded wrath), they were more like wild animals than human beings; not that they suspected the girls any more than anyone else, but they knew that they were secretly being laughed at by the perpetrator of this awful joke, and that was more than they could stand.

It was not long, however, before the whole matter was cleared up, thanks to the efforts of a detective who made the necessary investigations at the stores, was given the letters Retta had written to them — signed illegibly — and with the help of a handwriting expert had little trouble in tracing these documents back to their brazen author. My mother was called to the directress's office where she indignantly denied the charges preferred against her daughter, whereupon the latter was summoned and proudly pleaded guilty to everything. She was so cool and unafraid of consequences that it seemed useless to rebuke her in any way, but she left the Lycée Molière that afternoon in spite of the fact that her victims, who could not help loving her, insisted that she was amply forgiven, as far as they were concerned; nevertheless, it was felt that an example had to be made.

56

Years went by before I was told why Retta had been expelled from school and, of course, I dared not ask her. I loved her, but she awed me a little as she did all of us. The thought of opposing her in any way was completely foreign to me. In my eyes, she was right in everything she did and I dimly felt that she belonged to a superior race of human beings to whom fear was unknown: nothing ever seemed to make her flinch or cower; there was boldness in her eye and unconquerable obstinacy in her brow, and with it all the kindest of hearts.

The 14th of July, Bastille Day, was a national holiday and brought the last school term to a close. Two days before, there was a general awarding of prizes to the best students, a ceremony which, at all other *lycées*, took place in the school buildings. We were so numerous at Janson, however, that it was thought more convenient to gather us in one of the largest public buildings in Paris, the old Trocadéro palace, whch was pulled down in nineteen-thirty-seven.

Everybody agrees that from the point of view of architecture, the Trocadéro was an eyesore. It was built in Moorish style with two lofty minarets; the stone used was an ugly brown with blue majolica ornaments here and there, which did not make matters any better. The hall inside was everything the outside led one to expect, huge and

57

hideous with a decided oriental effect created by silk draperies and arched windows. Popular concerts were given in that dreadful place, but the acoustics were so peculiar that it was difficult to know where to sit and not hear the echo which faithfully repeated the whole program from start to finish. At the back of the stage was a gigantic organ, far more impressive when it was silent than when it pealed forth, because of its dismal want of repair.

However, the Trocadéro was considered good enough for us boys to sit in and be given our prizes, and at any rate it contained us all. As we trooped into the hall on the twelfth of July, we were greeted by solemn croakings from the organ and went to our seats in perfect order, under the eyes of the whole faculty assembled on the stage, hundreds of professors in their black and purple robes, deans dressed from head to foot in bright yellow silk, and the directors in crimson gowns trimmed with ermine. Over to the right was a sort of oasis made of the largest palms that could be obtained, back of which sat a military band ready to play. It makes me feel tremendously old to remember that the soldiers were dressed in red and blue uniforms — *pioupious,* we called them in those days — old and a little sad too, because a few years later those same uniforms were to be seen only too plainly on the battle-fields of France.

Parents and students sat together, the latter wearing white cotton gloves for the occasion. Presently the band

58

would strike up from behind the oasis and everybody rose to hear that strange and beautiful piece of music, the *Marseillaise*; after which, we all sat down and a gentleman in a black coat, whom no one had noticed at first, would draw some papers out of his pocket, advance towards the center of the stage, look right and left as if he hadn't really expected to see anyone in the hall, and begin.

I have never been partial to speeches, sermons or lectures. The spoken word has the same lulling effect on me as I have noticed it has on a great many people. If I were very rich and suffered from insomnia, I think that I should hire a professional after-dinner speaker to send me gently to sleep with a monotonous flow of anecdotes. To return to the gentleman in black, all I can accurately recall about him is that he was terribly reminiscent. He called us his "young friends" in a patronizing sort of way and usually admitted at the very start, as a proof of great humility, that he too had been a small boy, incredible though it might seem now, that he too had attended school and been made to struggle through a primer, nay, that he had even been made to stand in a corner with his face to the wall and a paper cap on his head (laughter and a certain amount of polite applause somewhat muffled by those white cotton gloves; the gentleman smiles and proceeds . . .).

Sometimes, the speaker was a member of the faculty and sometimes a well-known writer or a member of the bar.

One year, a rather shabby looking man addressed us. His long hair was untidily brushed back, his accent far from the cultured, oily tones we were accustomed to; in fact, he sounded more like a plumber or a coachman; but it was not long before we hung on every word he said, although he seemed to have little to impart: his name was Aristide Briand.

As a rule, however, the speaker was anything but entrancing and never tired of talking about himself. Such being the case, it was a comfort to think that even though I had to sit still, nothing in the world could compel me to listen, and I didn't; neither did anyone else. At last there was a salvo of applause indicating that the bore was through and the band would strike up lustily. Now came the exciting moment when two or three professors from the lower forms would take up their places behind a long table covered with books. Why we were so excited about these books, I do not know, because they always turned out to be extremely dull and we knew it beforehand, but they were our prizes and we wanted them. Sheer vanity, I suppose.

Presently, a member of the faculty would rise and begin reading the names of the best scholars in the higher forms: Philosophy and Rhetoric, and a few lanky, bespectacled lads of sixteen or seventeen shyly ascended the red velvet steps leading to the platform. There were always one or two among them who came down again with so many gilt-edged volumes in their arms that it seemed reasonable enough to hope that they would fall headlong down the red velvet steps; all the funnier, we thought, since each had been presented with a laurel wreath which he wore on his learned brow. But nothing of the sort ever happened; they picked their way back to their seats amid general applause.

Next came the boys in second, third and fourth grades whose names were read rather faster, thus creating a slight confusion, but the right boys always seemed to get the books and the laurel wreaths in the end and there was a brief intermission from time to time, which allowed everything to be nicely straightened out; the band played snatches from operas and the professors in charge of the prizes mopped their brows and had a short rest.

The latter part of the ceremony was gone through with somewhat of a rush. We smaller boys were not considered very interesting and lunch hour was getting near enough to make everyone a little restless. Nevertheless, nothing really went wrong and I regret to say that the only hitch that ever occurred was caused by me. I have tried to live it down, but somehow the memory of such things will not die, and I can never hear the overture to *Carmen* without wincing.

This is what happened. But I must first explain that school prizes in France fall into three categories: first prize, second prize and a strange thing called *accessit* which is really a delusion and a snare (or so it was to me), because although one's name is called out for an *accessit,* no tangible reward is offered, and it is considered wiser not to ask for one. Unfortunately, I was terribly misinformed on such matters when I was twelve; moreover, I was a foolish, gullible person, as will appear.

Not being a very hard working student, I seldom if ever got any prize, and that year I expected none. However, when my class was mentioned, I pricked up my ears and listened hopefully; to my great surprise, my name was called out. True it was called out after everybody else's and at the very bottom of the list of various subjects: French, English, German, Mathematics, History, and so forth. It was in connection with drawing that my name was mentioned. I did not excel in this subject, but my efforts had nevertheless been rewarded with an *accessit.*

An *accessit!* How exciting! A mischievous boy who sat by me and saw my flurry, asked me if I wasn't going up to get my *accessit.* I said a word to my mother (who had no idea of what an *accessit* might be), hastily put on my gloves which I had taken off because of the heat, and made my way down the aisle. As we sat in the middle of the row, quite a number of people had to be disturbed to let me pass, and I did not have any time to waste before the dreaded intermission took place.

So I hurried up the red velvet steps and exchanged smiles with my fat friend Simonin who was bearing away a stack of bulky red books. With his round pink cheeks and his laurel wreath on his head, he looked like a sacrificial pig on a Roman bas-relief which was reproduced in our history book, but I was too pressed for time to tell him so. Besides, it seemed to me that there were precious few books left on the table and I was quite out of breath when I gave my name.

"How do you spell your name?" asked the nervous little man without looking at me. I spelled it. "Louder, please!" I spelled it louder. He fumbled among the books for a moment and found nothing. Meanwhile, my classmates were going back to their seats and I was left on the platform with the faculty and the brass band. "My young friend, there must be some mistake. Are you sure you belong to this class? Let us look among the others." He did, conscientiously, but found nothing. By this time, the band master had already begun showing signs of unrest, as the band was not supposed to strike up before everybody was seated. I was therefore being eyed with extreme disfavor and the nervous little man, whose business it was to find a book for me, soon became frantic with irritation. "It's inconceivable that a prize should have been forgotten. I shall

63

certainly complain to the librarian," he muttered. "Tell me what your prize is for. Louder, please!"

I then told him it was an *accessit* for drawing. He gave an hysterical squeal. "*Comment!*" he said. "Do you mean to tell me that you are asking for an *accessit* to carry away under your arm? With illustrations, I suppose, and a ribbon around it. Young man, are you laughing at *us*?"

There was something so solemn and ominous about that last question that I felt my knees tremble and I moved away in horror. Hardly had I reached the top of the steps when Bizet's triumphant music crashed forth and with a burning face I scuttled down the aisle.

My mother was a little puzzled but sympathetic. She explained, as we left the Trocadéro, that such errors often occurred and that the important thing in the present case was that my name had been called out. The rest, she went on, didn't amount to a row of pins.

However, I thought differently on the subject and had to be taken to a nearby pastry-shop, where I derived a reasonable amount of moral comfort from a *baba au rhum* and a pistachio ice cream.

Although we were made to read our Bible every day and learned the thirty-nine articles by heart, we were not taken to church as regularly as might have been expected. This was due to the fact that my father was a Presbyterian* and my mother an Episcopalian, and their churches were not represented in Paris. There was, of course, the non-denominational church in the avenue de l'Alma, but in trying to be a little of everything, that is, in trying to suit everybody's taste, it was, my mother contended, neither one thing nor the other. Nevertheless, she liked the service and attended it with us once or twice a month, but she also took us to the English Church which she thought nearer to her own in spirit.

One Sunday morning, my father declared that we didn't go to church often enough and that his children were growing up like heathens.

"Well," said my mother, "why don't *you* take them to church for a change?"

* My father became a Catholic in 1915.

65

"Indeed I will. I'll take them to *my* church."

"Your church, Edward?"

"Certainly. That is, the nearest approach to my church. The French Protestant Church, in the rue Cortambert."

"Oh."

That was all my mother said. She was lying in bed, that morning, with a bad headache and for her to accompany us was out of the question, but she probably thought that low church was better than no church, and closing her eyes she tried to go back to sleep.

Meanwhile, my father finished dressing and sprayed himself with Russian Eau de Cologne. He was a tall, handsome man, with a dark complexion and beautiful kind brown eyes. His bushy eyebrows and heavy moustache gave him a somewhat fierce appearance, and my mother used to say that he would make a first-class bandit, except that he dressed more carefully than people of that profession usually do. No spots were ever to be seen on his clothes and the crease in his trousers was invariably perfect. He was always in a good temper and never had a cross word for anyone, but of course there were a few things in this world that did occasionally put him in a rage and I have seen him stamp his foot at the mere thought of them, the Dreyfus case, for instance.

To come back to that Sunday morning, I think I can truly say that, in those days at least, my father was not what is called a church-goer, but he made it clear that he did not want his children to grow up like heathens, so having told us to put on our hats and coats, he went into the hall, put on his own coat and reached for his top hat.

This was the very hat which I had endeavored to offer up. It was a very handsome silk hat, a shiny silk hat which shone even more if one stroked it lightly with the small brown velvet cushion I have already mentioned. And that is precisely what my father did before placing it on his head: he stroked with the brown velvet cushion. And then, *en avant, marche*! we trooped off, leaving my mother to her darkened room.

The Protestant Church in the rue Cortambert was as austere as Calvin himself could have desired. The walls were bare, the window panes were made of white glass, and it was decidedly a mortification of the flesh to sit in the pews. However, I don't suppose we had been brought to church to be comfortable, and it was of no use for the heathens to rage about it. We sat, I remember, in an upper gallery from which we obtained a fair view of the ladies' hats and of the preacher's bald spot as that worthy man ascended the pulpit.

First a hymn was sung and, as was natural, sung in French, which made us all feel curiously self-conscious and uncomfortable, because we always associated religion with the English tongue. It was entirely my father's idea to take

67

us to a French service, that morning, whereas, hitherto, we had attended only English-speaking churches. What a disastrous idea it turned out to be, I hope soon to make clear.

So the congregation stood and sang a hymn about Canaan, our heavenly home, and we, not knowing the words, kept silent. Now my father was last in our row, having gone in first and I stood by him. What to do with my hat soon became a problem, because it was one of those large straw hats with a turned up brim which children were made to wear in those days, and there was no room for it under the pew; after fingering it nervously for a while, I decided to do what my father did with his: I placed it behind me, on the seat.

Meanwhile, the singing of the hymn about Canaan proceeded and verse after verse rang out. It was a very long hymn and not a word was omitted, as I had occasion to ascertain when a hymn-book was placed in my hands by my father. I felt too shy to sing with the rest of the congregation, yet I was terribly afraid not to behave like everyone else; these mixed feelings made me unhappy and a little nervous.

We were about to reach the last verse when a gentleman who had come in late asked us in a loud whisper if we could not make room for him in our pew. My sisters and I were singularly lacking in initiative and the only thing we could think of was to look at each other, which we did, but my father grasped the situation immediately and made signs to us to move up. He moved up himself, holding his book in both hands, then I moved up, also holding my book, then each of my sisters, and finally the gentleman was able to get into our pew, which he did after having bowed politely to my father, who returned the bow.

By this time, the congregation had sung their way right through the hymn and sat down to listen to the sermon. We too sat down, uneasily.

It was at least a minute before I fully realized that something dreadful had happened. I didn't want to realize it. I struggled with myself and refused to face an unbelievable fact. I wanted everything to be all right, as it was a moment before; I did not want to believe that I was sitting on my father's top hat.

It wasn't, it couldn't be true. To begin with, if it had been true, would my father be calmly sitting by me, with his hands on his knees, listening to a sermon? Not daring to move, I remained seated and kept as quiet as I could. My hat, by the way, was on my sister Lucy's lap; she had wisely picked it up before sitting down, and with woe in my heart I wished that I had been as thoughtful as she. Presently she nudged me and asked where Papa's hat was. I pretended not to hear, whereupon the question was repeated in a louder whisper. I inwardly cursed her curiosity and told her to be quiet, but the reason why she was so

69

inquisitive was that she suspected the truth, which I finally revealed to her.

Our whispering annoyed our father who glared at us as savagely as he could, thus striking terror in my soul but by no means impressing Lucy; on the contrary, she was seized with a fit of uncontrollable laughter which she tried to suppress by stuffing her handkerchief into her mouth, and of course Anne and Retta began laughing too for no definite reason except that laughter is contagious among the very young. I alone remained steeped in horrible gloom and felt like a man about to be guillotined.

Now there is an end to everything, even to a Calvinist sermon, and the time came for us to rise and listen to another hymn before leaving. So we rose, I very reluctantly. After which there were prayers and, I suppose, more hymns, but all I can remember distinctly is that my father suddenly uttered a low groan as he happened to look back.

The next thing that stands out in my memory is a young boy being made to run alongside of a hatless and irate gentleman in a frock coat, down the rue Cortambert, then down the rue Guichard, finally up the rue de Passy. Three little girls follow behind, trying to keep pace, which they no doubt find difficult as the gentleman appears to be in a great hurry.

When we reached home, I burst into my mother's room and without a word of explanation disappeared under her bed, nor did she have time to ask for an *éclaircissement* before my father came in with a walking stick in his hand and, I imagine, a very ominous countenance. This last point I was not in a position to ascertain, but I took it for granted, and I did see the end of the walking stick. Thereupon a dialogue ensued which sounded like the conversation between the ogre and his wife in Perrault's fairy tale:

"Where is that boy?"

"Why, Edward, what on earth is the matter?"

"He is hiding in this room, I know it."

"But what has he done?"

Then, with a roar and a stamp, my father revealed the truth to my mother, who listened in shocked silence. When she had recovered she pleaded for me, but it was all useless and this scene was brought to a painful climax over which I may be allowed to draw a veil.

My friend Jean Simonin, to whom I recounted this story on the following Thursday, did not prove at all sympathetic; on the contrary, he laughed and said it served me right for going to an heretical church, whereupon I pulled his nose and he tried to kill me with his Latin dictionary (Quicherat, Daveluy et Chatelain).

This controversy, which took place in the Simonin's dining room, was interrupted by the sudden arrival of Jean's mother who appeared on the scene in a pale blue

71

dressing-gown and waved a fat bare arm above her son's head. She was a short, stoutish woman, with masses of frizzly brown hair and merry little eyes in a round dimpled face; her smiles and the heavy odor of heliotrope which accompanied her ingratiated this lady in my eyes, and I bemoaned the fact that I never saw her except for a few brief minutes at tea time, when she poured out glasses of thick red syrup for me and for Jean and offered us some of those crackers known as *petits beurres* out of an ugly glass jar made in the shape of a basket.

Once every two weeks, on Thursdays, I was invited to spend the afternoon at Jean's flat and on the stroke of four to partake of the refreshments I have described. It was a matter of only a few minutes to go to the Simonins' home, as they lived almost across the street from us, just above a well-known pastry-shop called Petit's. From the dining-room window Jean and I could hear the Passy-Bourse rumble by and it was there, probably, that we caught our first sight of the much laughed at *femmes-cochères,* or women drivers. These worthy ladies made their appearance in the streets of Paris towards 1909, perched on the seats of the familiar black and yellow cabs, and were the butt of many rude jokes which they took with their native light-hearted-ness. One disrespectful song was sung about them, the first lines of which ran something like this:

> *Ce n'est pas une petite affaire*
> *D'être coco, d'être coco, d'être cochère!*
> *Qu'il fasse beau ou qu'il neige,*
> *Pas moyen d'quitter son siège!*

And so forth, but I am wandering from my subject and must return to the Simonins. Jean and I went to the same school; however, he was a much better scholar than I and carried off all those gilt-edged books on the twelfth of July, which gave him an immense superiority over me. His golden locks, blue eyes and round pink cheeks did much to gain him the reputation of being a good child, not to say an angel, and he was held up to me as an example; but if truth had been known, he was a bully and liked me as only a bully can like his victim. Having grown wiser about such matters, I realize today that I was what the French call his *souffre-douleur,* his favorite *souffre-douleur* whom he could mentally browbeat at a very small cost because I was then easily impressed by a show of knowledge. He excelled at inventing answers to hard questions and knew precisely what manner of expression and what tone of voice would win my approbation. Of course, being an ingenuous person, I was not aware of such subtleties and listened round-eyed to his outrageous lies. One day he took a piece of mala-

73

chite from a what-not in his parents' drawing room and
gave me to believe, which I immediately did, that it had
been presented to his father by his friend the Tsar of Russia, whose life Monsieur Simonin had saved on a winter
night when they both happened to be walking through
the woods together and a bear had attacked Nicholas II.
Why they were walking through the woods together on a
winter night was not very clear, but I was not critical of
such a good story and asked for more details, which were
added forthwith. Later, I discovered that Monsieur Simonin kept a chemist store near the Gare Montparnasse,
which did not tally very well with Jean Simonin's account
of him, and I was troubled with doubts as to my school-
mate's truthfulness, but it took several years really to shake
my belief in his word.

Like every Frenchman of his generation, Jean Simonin
wrote his *devoirs* and studied his lessons at the dining-room
table, a green baize cover being placed on that piece of
furniture for the occasion. Even on Thursdays he was expected to translate a page or so from the *De Viris* or work
out one of those diabolical train problems in which two
locomotives starting from the same point, covering the
same number of kilometers and running at different speeds,
reach their destination at the same time in spite of logic or
reason (so I thought), but in strict accordance with our
professor's views. There was another problem too, in which

74

a clever and determined Greek boy succeeded in growing older than his father in his father's lifetime. Jean Simonin could solve these hideous riddles with comparative ease, while I groaned over them and passed from a state of acute irritation to one of quiet despair, finally handing in a paper which was returned to me with a zero. In fact, so many of my papers were returned to me with that grade that my sisters called me Monsieur Zéro.

On alternate Thursdays, Jean Simonin came to our house where he spent the hours between two and six. This he enjoyed even more thoroughly than when I came to play with him, because, being a guest, he was in a better position to bully me. He would tear sheets out of my copybooks and turn them into *cocottes,* i.e., paper chickens, which he would send flying into Monsieur Cassagnade's garden, regardless of the fact that my copy-books were thus woefully mutilated and that Monsieur Cassagnade objected to the presence of *cocottes* in his neat enclosure. Or else he would gallop noisely through the house when he knew that my mother was out; or he would lean out of the drawing-room window and spit on the passers-by's hats, timing it with such admirable precision that he hardly ever missed his target. "Do you see that old lady with black straw hat? Now watch me . . ." I watched and drew back in horror as Jean, with shrieks of mirth, pointed at the black straw hat moving away unconscious of anything wrong. Sometimes I tried to pull Jean into the room, but he merely kicked back like a mule and refused to budge. He was far stronger than I: his arms felt like stone and his vigorous bare calves bulged out of his tightly laced boots. However, he knew when to be meek and spoke to my mother with a mild voice, even managing to blush when complimented, which made him seem attractively shy; but no sooner was my mother out of the room than he would jump on my back and roar:

"Now, Aeneas, carry your father Anchises out of flaming Troy!"

I would immediately throw him on the rug where we scrambled madly for the next few minutes, but he always got the better of me and ended by planting his heel on my stomach as he recited a line from Vergil. He was something of a pedant and I took it for granted that he would rise to great heights.

Some years ago he called on me. "I remembered your address," he said. "I thought I would drop in for a moment. Yes, it's been over twenty years, hasn't it? I suppose I have changed a little, oh, yes, I have. I weigh a hundred and eighty and most of my hair is gone, but what do I care? I have a small pharmacy near the Gare Montparnasse and make a good living. Why don't you look me up some day and we'll talk over old times. Latin? No. I've forgotten every word. It's of no practical use except to understand a few medical terms. All I am interested in now is drugs and pills. . . ."

Thus did Jean Simonin the man kill Jean Simonin the boy in a short speech of seven lines.

CHAPTER EIGHT

Towards the 10th of July, the family trunk was hauled up from the cellar and placed in my mother's bedroom. It was a large, cumbersome affair made of osier and creaked distressingly when my mother opened it, but I loved the sound of it because it meant that the long summer holiday was at hand. Today I wonder how we managed to put everything we needed for two months and a half in one trunk, but I know that it was done; it was one of those miracles of family life that go unrecorded. We were five children. When the trunk was filled to capacity, two or three of us were called in to sit on the lid and bear down on it with all the strength and weight we could command; we complied zealously while my father worried the locks, bit his tongue and grew red in the face as he struggled with the key. Then of course there was always something which had been forgotten and paper parcels had to be made up, but nobody minded; we were all too happy.

How small our trunk looked once it had been hoisted

up on the driver's box! My mother got into one cab with her three youngest children, while Eleanor and Mary sat a little scornfully in another cab with my father; then off to the Saint Lazare station! By the time we had reached that grimy building, we were in such a state of excitement that we began acting, as children do, like lunatics, jumping up and down and trying to dismember my mother by pulling at her arms. She, being a nervous woman, was distracted by harrowing thoughts which she expressed aloud with wails of despair: "Have I left the gas burning in the kitchen? Did I leave without giving the concierge the keys to the flat? Did I really turn off the water in the bathroom after washing my hands? I can't remember packing the children's underwear. Their sandals! I've forgotten their wretched sandals!" And so forth until we were thrown into a sort of panic; but as soon as we were in the train, everything seemed to be all right again, and it didn't matter whether anything had been left behind, because we were all together, making our way through the gloomy suburbs and eagerly watching out for the first signs of country, the first fields, the first cows resting in the shade of trees.

Our summer house was an old-fashioned villa on the banks of the Seine, not quite an hour from Paris. To my dying day, I shall remember the red roof, the heavy green shutters, the colored glass door in the hall, and the musty

79

smell of the rooms that had remained shut up all winter. There was a long terraced garden overlooking the river, with a row of magnificent elms on the opposite bank, a simple landscape but one that is very near my heart. The happiness of childhood, I know full well, is impossible to describe and I shall not attempt it, but even as I write about our holidays, something of the old feeling seems to come back, the joy unmixed with any thought of the sadness, or fear, or regret which so often mar the joy of manhood. Day after day went by bringing nothing but pleasure; headaches and boredom, the gift of later years, were unknown to us and the sun always set sooner than we should have wished.

Indeed it was not without a certain feeling of unrest that I saw night coming on, as going to bed was something of an ordeal. There were no gas-fixtures on the upper floors and I was given a candle to light my way through the dark. This took place shortly after eight and I lingered as long as possible in the drawing-room, bidding everyone good night several times over, in an attempt to defer the dreaded moment when I should have to go through the hall and upstairs.

The hall was dimly lit by a hurricane lamp placed on a table near the foot of the steps, but an additional quantity of light came from a crack in the drawing-room door which I was careful to leave ajar when I went out. It was seldom noticed that the door had not been closed, and with luck it remained in that condition for hours at a time. I sat on a step half-way up the staircase, having first extinguished my candle, waiting for the moment to come when everyone would go to bed and I could face the horror of a pitch black room to which I scampered as soon as I heard my father say: "Well, I think I'll turn in."

When my mother tiptoed into the room to undress for the night, I was, of course, sound asleep, or so it appeared. Now I cared very little whether I had light or darkness around me: my mother's bed was only ten feet away from mine and I knew that nothing in the world could harm me. But it was different when I sat on those steps and watched the shadows cast on the ceiling by the hurricane lamp. Only a child can realize to the full what it means to fancy one sees or hears something moving and breathing in the dark. This was my experience every night and to it alone can I ascribe that strange prominence given to staircases in most of my novels, in connection with any great distress of mind undergone by my characters.

To be sure, the crack in the drawing-room door was a tremendous comfort, but it sometimes happened that this door was closed after I had left the room; all I could do then was hastily light my candle, if I had put it out, and try to keep up my spirits by reading a small copy of La Fontaine's fables, which I had slipped under my arm, and by not paying attention to what I feared went on behind me.

Somehow, my sister Mary found me out. Instead of telling on me, however, as a less kindhearted person might have done, she managed to have the drawing-room door left open a little wider and played softly on the piano. She had come back from a long trip to Italy some time before and brought back a number of popular songs which she rendered to the best of her ability, not attempting, however, anything more than humming as she accompanied herself on a rather tinny Steinbeck. I listened to this music from my place of hiding with a feeling of deep gratitude. One of the songs, I remember, bore the title of *Tripoli* and was sung by the unfortunate Italian soldiers who were then being sent to Libya. Other songs were of a more peaceful character and described moonlight effects on Mediterranean waters. I liked everything indiscriminately.

All nightly fears were, of course, forgotten in the morning, and except for one brief half-hour I had nothing to do but to play until sundown. My mother was too humane a person to spoil my holidays by making me study, as so many French children were made to do, but she did insist on teaching me a little English every day. So I read to her from a brown backed primer and she listened patiently to dull stories about Saint Bernard dogs rescuing travelers in the snow or prisoners making their escape with a file hidden in a loaf of bread. No doubt my pronunciation grated on her ear, but she was long-suffering with her last-born and corrected him gently, whereas my sisters, who studied a more advanced form of English under her care, were more often than not "given back the book," which meant, in her parlance, that the book was thrown at their heads. There was nothing of the school-ma'am about her. She tried to make us love English as much as she did and was intolerant of slovenly speech, having herself an exquisite sense of verbal precision and aptness of phrase.

Naturally enough, I suppose, she was anxious to make us read some of the books she had enjoyed in her salad days, but here the conflict between two generations became acute: we balked at Bulwer-Lytton and Scott and looked so miserable while reading those venerable bores that she took the books away from us indignantly and called us Yahoos. However, I did get through *Ivanhoe,* but I had to be bribed into doing this; I was promised ten *sous* if I could report intelligently on that novel. Being hard up for pocket money, I accepted, but when one realizes that ten *sous* is just half a franc, it must be admitted that I was not overpaid. Nor did anything good come of that reading which put it into my head to abduct Coucou Blanc as Front-de-Boeuf abducted Rebecca, with dramatic results in both cases.

English was certainly my mother's best means of expressing herself, but, like Teddy Roosevelt, she spoke French with "daring fluency." Grammar was never known to have stopped her and she disregarded genders with superb indifference, but she spoke as quickly as any French woman of her day and always made her meaning clear. Her accent and the wild liberties she took with the language were sources of merriment for all her friends, and there is an instance when she made a whole courtroom rock with laughter as she was called upon to testify in a civil law suit. She laughed immoderately herself, having a fine sense of humor, and went ahead undaunted and untrammeled.

Although her health was far from perfect, she never allowed it to interfere with what she considered her duties or to cast a shadow over our happiness. We were too young to realize that she was ill, and she was too gay to mind. Her fondness for telling jokes was thwarted by her inability to remember the point of a story, which made her laugh all the more. Her bright, optimistic nature gave us all a sense of well-being and her presence seemed as necessary to me as light itself.

Nothing in the world could make me happier than to go out walking hand in hand with her or to sit by her as we drove through the country in François' carriage. François was a handsome boy of twenty who took us out once or twice a week in an old-fashioned victoria and showed as much of the *département de Seine et Oise* as we cared to see for the sum of five francs. The name of our village was Andrésy. It was one of the oldest settlements in that part of France and went back to the times when Rollon the Norseman raided the banks of the Seine. Like so many villages in France, it was an epitome of the country's history from the dark ages up to the days of Louis-Philippe or thereabout, as, for some reason, life in Andrésy seemed to have come to a standstill around 1840. I am afraid this is no longer true today, and what we are pleased to call progress has made its way into the remotest parts of France, but in 1910 or 12 automobiles were not seen in Andrésy, telephones were scarce and seldom used, candlelight still held in honor. If any discomfort was caused by this, we were not sensible of it and in any case it was amply compensated for by something which our so-called civilization has lost for many years: I mean quiet, serenity and a sort of inner contentedness. There was peace in the medieval streets of Andrésy, not the blare of radios extolling the merits of hair oil or baking powder. However, I may as well be frank: there *was* a moving-picture theater.

It wasn't really a moving-picture theater. Moving pictures were then considered childish, something like a sort of glorified magic lantern, and it would no doubt have been thought absurd to build a theater for the purpose of sheltering this new toy, but a room could be let where performances might be given for the entertainment of the young. Monsieur Nicole had such a room. He owned a restaurant where banquets and wedding breakfasts were arranged; above the restaurant, on the second floor of a long cream-colored house, was what he pompously termed the *salle des fêtes*, a large bare room with straight chairs along the wall; here balls were occasionally given and once or twice a year, during the first week in August, a moving-picture show was put on.

Several days ahead, the main street of Andrésy was placarded with theater bills in which capitals and exclamation marks played a prominent part. The program was extremely copious, or so it seemed at first glance, eight or nine films being given of an evening. I can still remember with what eagerness we read the titles of these films, each one of which was followed by a descriptive adjective the purpose of which was to whet our appetite. One program, I recall, ran something like this:

1. Cyrano's Madrigal.
   (artistic)

2. A Mother's Ordeal.
   (sentimental)

3. The Fatal Woman.
   (dramatic!)

86

4. The Dance of the Flowers.
   (graceful and artistic)

5. The Fireman's Wedding.
   (comical! !)

6. Murder at the Mill.
   (very dramatic! ! People with weak hearts are advised to stay away.)

Finally came *La Course aux Potirons* (The Pumpkin Race), which was described as *désopilant* or side-splitting, with a whole row of exclamation marks.

My younger sisters and I were delirious with joy at the thought of so much pleasure in store and we simply did not know how to wait for the grand evening to come. Days crept by and at long last the moment arrived when we were told to put on our hats to go to the cinema. From our house to Monsieur Nicole's Restaurant was about five minutes' walk along the river, under a double row of sweet smelling linden trees. I was afraid that, no seats having been booked, there might not be room enough for all seven of us, but it always turned out very well and we were seated in the fourth or fifth row. These were the expensive seats: ten sous apiece. The mayor, the grocer and their families sat with us, also the notary who was a single gentleman. Back of us giggled the village beaux and their girls. Newspaper had been pinned over the windows. The screen was an ordinary sheet hung on a rope. An upright piano was placed nearby, at which a lady sat with a shy grin on her face, waiting. Presently Monsieur Nicole extinguished the gas chandelier and we were plunged in Egyptian darkness, whereupon cat-calls and pig-like grunts came from the back of the room, accompanied by shrill feminine laughter. Then a noise was heard which sounded like grains of sand striking a pane of glass and a rather uncertain light was cast on the screen. At that moment, the pianist struck up with a joggy tune and I opened my eyes as wide as I could, but all I could discern on the screen was something that looked like rain. We all had the same experience. However, if you looked long enough, and tried to forget about the little black specks on the screen, you began to see a gesticulating silhouette, a man with a long nose and a long rapier. It was wonderful! He actually moved about, opened his mouth and placed his hand over his heart while he gazed at a lady on a balcony. All of a sudden, a voice was heard, that of Monsieur Nicole's son-in-law who was good enough to oblige and sang Gounod's serenade with something of a bleat while the pianist fumbled through the accompaniment as best she could. By drawing on one's imagination, it was almost possible to fancy that the voice belonged to the man on the screen, except that he opened his mouth a little out of time; on the whole it was a beau-

88

tiful performance and, as the program had guaranteed, artistic.

There was loud applause and a brief intermission, after which came the story of a lady whose little boy was taken from her by her divorced husband; she waved her arms and tore savagely at her hair. Every time the wicked husband appeared the piano rumbled angrily, and an appropriate "berceuse" was played when the child was shown asleep in his bed with his long hair done up in a sissy knot. The rest of the time, however, the piano remained silent so as to allow the commentator to explain the story and once in a while put in a line or two of dialogue. ("My child. . ." "He is no longer your child, Madame, the hand of the law has given him to me." "Monsieur, you are killing me!" *"Mes hommages,* Madame. Come, Victor!") And so the eye, the ear and the intellect were equally satisfied.

By the time we reached *Murder at the Mill,* things began to go a little wrong. The pianist complained that she did not have enough light and a candle was brought, which somewhat spoiled the effect of the film, and the pianist was booed, whereupon, being a temperamental person, she blew out the candle and left in a huff. Shortly after that, the machine broke down and had to be hastily mended while the villagers hissed and stamped; they were becoming more and more critical as the evening wore on and be-

gan laughing at the dramatic moments, which showed, I
suppose, the awakening of the modern spirit. I buried my
face in my mother's shoulder when the villain slit the miller's neck with a kitchen knife and the commentator made
a realistic gurgling sound. What with Cyrano's serenade,
the Mother's Ordeal and the Dance of the Flowers, I was
feeling sleepy and wanted to go home.

The last picture, however, seemed to rally everyone in
the room. It has become famous in the annals of French
cinema and I can affirm that to a crowd of 1912 *La Course
aux Potirons* appeared irresistibly funny. I suppose the
public was more ingenuous in those days. To see large
pumpkins rolling down a very steep street in Montmar-
tre, upsetting carts and people as they went, evidently appealed to a sense of humor which we have lost or perverted.
In 1939, some of these old pictures were shown in New
York; the comical ones hardly drew a titter from the *blasé*
spectators, whereas dramas which had made me weep co-
piously in years gone by brought the house down.

I don't remember what my parents thought of the
show, but I wish that their opinion of it could have been
recorded, as a distance of thirty years might have lent it
something like historical interest. I do recall that I went
to bed and dreamt of the miller's mangled remains being
brought out of the river, where the murderer had thrown
them, by an avenging mill-wheel.

90

A little while ago I mentioned the victoria in which we were taken out to drive once or twice a week. These drives have remained fixed in my memory whereas longer and possibly more interesting excursions have faded, because it was on the heights overlooking Andrésy that I first conceived a definite idea of the beauty of France.

After passing the old village church, we went up a short, narrow street and found ourselves almost immediately in the fields. Then began the rough part of the journey along a stony road which meandered through vast expanses of wheat and barley practically as far as the eye could travel. On days when the sky was overcast and the wind blew down into the valley of the Seine, these fields, surging and billowing like the sea, afforded a sight of incredible loveliness. A few miles below, the river gleamed, skirting ancient woods where Frankish armies had encamped. So much in this landscape suggested history that the soul of France seemed to be crying out in the wind, singing one of those wild songs which the Roman invaders must have heard. Young though I was, I could not help being moved by this invisible and almost overpowering presence. I realized for the first time that France was not the name of an impersonal entity, a convenient way of designating a group of people within certain boundaries, but the self-given name of a living person, a great, strong and kindly being whose failings were surpassed by her generosity and courage; at times a creature of whims and sudden fancies, which led her astray, but in her better moments capable of wisdom and farsightedness; a soul of great spiritual wealth struggling with the temptation of earthly power and material well-being, a proud and valiant spirit. All this I felt in a dim sort of way, as a child can feel such things who has but small knowledge of history. Everything connected with the past of the French nation appealed to me very strongly. I remember, for instance, being stirred by the news that two Merovingian tombs had been discovered in the neighborhood of the railroad station at Andrésy: the long stone coffins were reverently placed in a nearby garden where I had a chance to look at them. What remained of the skeletons had been removed, together with two long, thin swords coated with green, but the rough-hewn sarcophagi spoke of times which I longed to have known, when the wolf and the auroch drank from the waters of the Seine and bronze-helmeted warriors smote their shields with the battle axe as they sang their war song.

Here then beat the heart of France, in these hills surrounding Paris. This was where she was born, l'Ile de France, where her first kings watched over her and led her to greatness. I loved her. In a picture book which my godmother had given me, France was represented in her early days as a child, later as a girl, then as a full grown woman with a proud and smiling countenance and a royal scepter in her hand; the thought that she would grow old and eventually die made me unhappy, but I hoped that I should never see that day. It pleased me to think that I spoke her language, that the very words I used were once heard in the streets of medieval Paris and that this link existed between France and me, who was not her son.

My mother shared with me this admiration for the country we lived in, but she never failed to remind me that I was an American, and as we looked at the scenery around us, she tried to make me understand in what respects it differed from what I might have seen in Virginia, for instance, my father's state. To begin with, each square foot of ground was cultivated. This, I think, is the most distinctive feature of almost any French landscape. There are no fences to mark the limits of the fields, a narrow path or a rut being usually considered sufficient. From afar, these dividing lines are of course invisible: wheat, oat, barley and vegetables grow in smallish fields apparently touching each other, the contrast between them being sometimes so sharp as to give the impression that a coat of many colors has been thrown over the shoulders of France, whereas an American landscape with its extensive fields and areas of uncultivated land is more uniform in tone. Then woods are sparse and fast disappearing in France: no French peasant can look at a tree without longing to cut it down and retrieve the soil it grows on. I believe it would be difficult to find in France the equivalent of an American forest with its wild underbrush and its eerie stillness, yet there was a time when Gaul from east to west was nothing but oaks and elms with hut villages in the clearings of this tremendous forest, traces of which are left at Fontainebleau and Compiègne.

All this my mother told me in the simplest words she could find, but I doubt that she gave me a very clear notion of the distant land she was endeavoring to describe. I could not rid myself of the idea that the United States looked something like a jungle with gigantic rivers whose brownish waters never reflected the face of heaven; it was an uncomfortable thought that there were so many snakes everywhere and that an alligator had almost been run over by a streetcar within the city limits of Savannah. Also I was a little dismayed by the fact that no building of great antiquity was to be seen in my mother's native land. My heart went out to the beautiful white churches around which the villages of France had clustered for more than ten centuries, and I wondered what a country could be like without them.

On Sundays, although not a Catholic, I was allowed to go to mass with some neighbors of ours, the Salvadors. Monsieur Salvador, being of a voltairian turn of mind, did not accompany us, but Madame Salvador and her daughter Jacqueline accepted me as an escort. They were French with some admixture of South American blood which came out strongly in the young girl whose olive complexion and liquid black eyes lent her an exotic kind of beauty; her glossy hair, her slender neck and delicate hands added much to her grace, and I went to play with her almost every afternoon under the watchful eye of her mother. The latter was far less attractive, but she made up for looks by dignity of bearing and had all the mannerisms of a pretty woman who, for some reason or other, does not wish to be courted. For all I know, she might well have been a raving beauty in the early days of the Third Republic, but as I remember her in 1912 ... Well, she was so stout that portions of her body bulged out of the wicker armchair in which she knitted as I played dominos with Jacqueline. A large beaky nose gave her face a somewhat ferocious expression which her plaited hair corrected to a certain

95

extent; dark, irregular liver spots covered her cheeks and wrinkled hands; she wore glasses with tortoise shell rims and spoke in a particularly luscious voice but never laughed. An offended stare was her reply to any kind of male attention which she considered suspicious; almost any compliment from a man was tainted in her eyes by some evil intent, for the simple reason that she looked upon herself as a sort of walking temptation for the stronger sex. This little *malentendu* was a source of great merriment for my elder sisters who boldly discussed the matter in my presence, thinking no doubt that I could not understand.

Be that as it may, I was in the Salvador's carriage a little before nine on Sunday mornings and off we drove. Jacqueline and I sat on the narrow *banquette* opposite Madame Salvador who wore what was then called a boa, or feather neckpiece, the tips of which fluttered gaily in the wind; her sallow cheeks were protected from the sun by a parasol held at a slant and, when closed, used as a means of cummunicating with the coachman by poking him in the back. There was something regal about Madame Salvador. To begin with, sheer weight made her impressive. When she stepped out of the carriage, that vehicle tipped to one side like a boat on a rough sea, and as she walked into the church people instinctively drew aside to make room for her. Being too portly to kneel before the altar, she gave a sort of curtsey and a polite nod in the middle of the aisle and having reached her place began wrestling with her *prie-Dieu* or high backed devotion chair, which she tilted forward as she threw the weight of her body on that creaking piece of furniture in an effort to take a reverent attitude without bending her legs more than was comfortable. Jacqueline knelt on her right and I on her left, aping Madame Salvador as closely as I could, not in a spirit of mockery, but anxious to make the right gestures at the right moment.

The church was fourteenth century although, like most country churches, built on earlier foundations. It smelt faintly of mustiness and more strongly of incense and flowers. The sun threw the pattern of the rose window on the high stone walls which were hung with ex-votos as far as a man's hand could reach. When the sermon was lengthy, I read these ex-votos, many of which I knew by heart. There seemed to be a peculiar fascination about them. It was interesting to know that Sophie Lanchantin, age 50, had broken her leg in the spring of '95 and had miraculously recovered the use of that limb after offering up a prayer at a certain altar in the church; that Lucienne Bompard had passed her examination in '81, in gratitude for which a tablet had been erected. Higher up, mention was made of Georges Payard who had come back safe and sound from the war of 1870, and of Adèle Groult whose life was spared in a railroad accident on the 18th of July

1887, and so forth. There were dozens of these little marble tablets, each one bringing to light one day in the lives of all these people, and it annoyed me to think that all the days that had come before as well as those that came after were forever enshrouded in darkness.

Madame Salvador followed the mass with great care in a thick little red book from which tiny pictures with paper lace borders occasionally dropped. Like the rest of the congregation she sang the *Credo* lustily, making the Latin words ring under the high Gothic vault much as they had done, century after century, in the very place where I stood. There was a strong appeal to my imagination in this thought. To be able to go back in time and in some curious way to find my place there, gave me a feeling of security which I am at a loss to explain and can only describe by saying that I delighted in fancying that I mingled with a medieval crowd. This perpetual harking back to the past, to a past which I had not known, was becoming a part of my mental makeup and worked powerfully on me in later years. However, as I stood by Madame Salvador and listened to her chaunting about the resurrection of the dead, and other articles of faith, I must confess that, quite apart from my flights of historical fancy, I was intent on another aspect of the ceremony at which I was assisting. It was the custom then, and still is in most parts of France, to offer the congregation small pieces of *brioche* or cake, as

98

a sort of symbolical communion. This "blessed bread" is distributed at high masses only and is carried in baskets by two choir boys in red cassocks and lace surplices. It is paid for by the wealthier members of the community, who consider it an honor to assume this expense each one in turn throughout the year. Thus it is announced from the pulpit that on the following Sunday, the *pain bénit* will be offered by Monsieur Nicole, who feels a slight glow of pride as his name is mentioned, or by Madame Lanchantin, who bridles in spite of herself. So shortly after the sermon, the bread is passed around the church. To anyone who has ever had a taste of French *brioche,* particularly before the first World War when everything seemed of a better quality, it will not sound surprising that I tried to get as large a portion of this heavenly food as could possibly be managed; but no sooner was the basket shoved under our noses by the impatient choir boy than I was confronted by the ever delicate problem of choosing. Each piece of *brioche* seemed to have an attractiveness of its own, some being of a golden brown, some the color of honey, and then there was a maddening difference in size and shape which rendered it all the more difficult to make up one's mind; I would choose one piece, drop it, take another, drop that, and finally, through sheer infirmity of purpose, pick what afterwards seemed to me the very smallest piece I could have found. Jacqueline, who was a bolder spirit and knew

99

her mind better than I did, managed to snatch an extra piece as the basket journeyed on its way *down* after having gone *up* our row, but I felt Madame Salvador's eye watching my hands and I simply didn't dare; however, I knew perfectly well what the Israelites experienced when they beheld the manna on the ground and I quite understand their desire to hoard it: I am sure it actually melted on the tongue, like *brioche*.

On the first foggy days of September, when the steamboats sounded hoarse, down the river, as they blew their whistle before reaching the sluice; when a fire had to be lit in the dining room and the bottle of red wine was placed on the floor at exactly the correct distance from the hearth, so that the flavor of the Medoc would be brought out to the full; when last year's shrunken flannels were sternly handed to us at the first sneeze and we had to struggle into this scratchy underwear, then was the time to feel sad and wonder at the flight of summer.

However, we lingered at Andrésy until it was too cold to stay with any pleasure. On the 25th or the 26th of September, we left. Why it was invariably fine on the day of our departure, I cannot tell, but it always looked as if the sky chose to be particularly bright and the trees particularly green as we drove to the station. "You're not going?" they seemed to say. "Why, summer is just beginning!" We sat in glum silence with parcels on our knees, hoping that François' carriage would break down or that his wheezy old mare would run away with us into the country, and that we would miss the train.

Nevertheless, it was exciting to go back to Paris. It is always exciting to go back to Paris, to watch the fields disappear one by one, and the houses grow dingier as they increase in number, to hurtle at top speed through suburban stations — "burning" stations, the French call that — burning Colombes, burning Asnières — how important it makes one feel to be burning all those stations and all of a sudden to read on a wall in gigantic letters: *Paris à 20 kilomètres,* twenty kilometers to Paris, then, after a few minutes, five hundred meters to Paris. Only think of it: five hundred meters to Europe's greatest city, as far as any small boy might walk, as far as he might run if he felt as eager as I did. It no longer mattered that the sky over Andrésy was blue and that the steamboats went by our house with their long barges, and we weren't there to watch them or wave at the fat lady at the helm and throw pebbles at the yelping fox-terrier, it no longer mattered because we were in Paris again, clambering into a cab with our wicker trunk fastened by a rope to the coachman's box (he stretched a protecting arm over it whenever it gave signs of slipping), then listening to our father as he named the various buildings we passed on our way to the rue de Passy, although we knew them quite well. How different his voice sounded as we rumbled through the crowded streets! It was not so clear as in the country where silence prevailed, but here, in the din of the city, somewhat indistinct, yet Papa's voice still, naming the Opéra, the Madeleine Church, the Place de la Concorde, then the unfortunate Grand Palais and Petit Palais which I ingenuously thought had been built in my honor, because these architectural atrocities had been erected in 1900.

By the first of October, the excitement of being in Paris again had died down and we were taken to school. Having reached the age of twelve, I was no longer made to wear the black alpaca apron which envelops every French child from neck to knees, or did in those distant years. I wore a starched turned down collar with a large lavallière bow and carried on my shoulders a leather bag much like a soldier's haversack. A dark blue cape which fastened tightly under my chin went over this leather bag and made me look, I was told, like Quasimodo, the humpback of Notre Dame, but I didn't care because thousands of boys in Paris were equipped in exactly the same way; like most children, I was a strict conformist.

Meeting the new boys and greeting last year's friends seemed to be the main function on October 1st, a pleasant one, all things considered, in spite of natural and spontaneous antipathies which found almost immediate expression. There always seemed to be a bully and a sneak in

103

every class, but they were spotted at once; all the other
boys were all right. Most of them were, of course, French,
but South Americans were numerous. We called them
rastas, short for *rastacouères.* Paris, in those days, swarmed
with rastas who came from Argentine and Brazil with
heavily brilliantined hair and that rich accent, so success-
fully imitated on the stage. At school, the Echavarrias, the
Da Conceçaos, the Salvadors and all the rest of them,
flocked together and jabbered in their native tongue; they
came to school in automobiles, displayed flashy ties and,
young though they were, wore sumptuous rings. Their
talk was decidedly grown-up and their fountain pens of
massive gold; no other ink than emerald green or blood
red was used by the members of this tribe. To say that they
were spoiled is mild; they were life's darlings. They were
much laughed at, but envied and, on the whole, quite
popular among us; their good nature and slightly ostenta-
tious generosity ingratiated them in our eyes; directly we
had passed the school gate, when classes were over, they
produced impressive gold cases, probably stolen from their
fathers, and offered us cigarettes which made us ill. None
of them knew French well, but it was supposed that they
would pick up a smattering of that language in the lower
forms; there was in consequence a difference of two or
three years between us, a fact which enhanced their pres-
tige beyond words in our opinion.

Our professors did not know very well how to cope with these boys. The latter, as a rule, were told to sit at the back of the room and few questions were asked them because they were impertinent fellows and answered back in such a way as to make us all giggle. When the grades were read out, once a month, they were named last and took it with a grin; one boy called Jauregui, a Peruvian with a fine Indian face, invariably brought up the rear as by a special and undisputed privilege.

Jewish boys topped the list. They understood all the problems, handed in the best compositions, and collected most of the prizes at the end of the year. There was no vying with them; they were far ahead of us and even offered to coach us during recreation hours. Mathematics, languages, literature, everything seemed to be their forte. On Saturdays, they were present like all of us, but quite a few among them abstained from writing; however, this did not in any way seem to retard them in their race to the fore.

Between the dark-skinned rastas and the curly-headed Jews, I and a few others fumbled along. Golden mediocrity appeared to be my lot. My conception of geometry was very distressing to old Monsieur Vacquant who shook his head in sorrow when I answered his questions at the blackboard. History amused me, but I did not approach it in the right spirit, remembering anecdotes and forgetting the dates. I enjoyed penciling what looked like brown caterpillars on maps where mountains were supposed to be indicated by the student, but I disliked geography otherwise. Neither was German my favorite study; I loathed its declensions and the strange way in which verbs were kicked all the way down long sentences until they dropped exhausted at the very end. In fact, I was less of a student than a sort of reluctant amateur and, as far as grades were concerned, came much nearer to our South American friends than to the curly-headed prodigies who headed the class.

It might be said in my defense that we were given too many things to study. Our leather bags were so full of books that fastening the prong of the buckle was a problem which could be solved only by brute force. They were excellent books and I only regret that I have forgotten so much of their contents. Nevertheless, I still believe that the gravest fault to be found with the French educational system of that period is that children's minds were overburdened with facts and not allowed to develop along their own lines. School hours were from eight to eleven in the morning (eight to twelve in higher forms) and from two to four in the afternoon. We were supposed to study from five to seven at home and indeed had to if we expected to keep up with the rest of the class (I never had such exalted hopes, however, and dropped out early in the day). The more zealous among us worked even after dinner, but doctors considered this unhealthy and I agreed with these learned men.

It can be gathered from what I have said that there was precious little time for play in this austere scheme of life. Jean Simonin, for instance, never had an opportunity to relax on week days, except on Thursday afternoons when he could disport himself at my expense until he was driven back to his books by a watchful and ambitious mother. When I think of French youth in those days, I invariably see a boy bent over a table stacked with books. How carefully he writes his *devoir,* his Latin themes and Greek exercises! At the age of fourteen he can read a page of Herodotus and find his way in the horrible chaos of the Hundred Years War. He can explain Newton's Theory of colors and knows the population of distant Russian cities; he is greatly in advance of most European boys, but I wonder if he is happy.

Jean Simonin with his pink cheeks and robust little body is the exception. Your average French boy of 1912 is apt to be wan and round-shouldered from over-work. Once a week, it is true, a professor of Gymnastics makes him do what is known as *exercices physiques,* i.e., rhythmically brandishing dumbbells, or climbing up a rope, all this fully dressed, of course; the idea of taking off one's clothes to go through exercises would be considered strange and indecent. So here is my little Frenchman touching the tips of his shoes with his stretched out fingers or swaying from side to side with his arms akimbo. Black stockings are pulled over his legs and his stiff collar pinches and strangles him as he stoops; but the brain is not all and the body must be exercised, according to medical authorities; so once a week, for one short hour, this French boy counts one two three four as he moves his arms and legs. He is certainly a brilliant student, but I wonder if he is strong.

To be sure, there are some people who think that the whole system of education is wrong and that the future of the French race is in danger if something isn't done to make the children healthier, but how can one give more time to gymnastics when there are so many things to learn? It is commonly said that the preceding generations of Frenchmen knew more Latin and studied longer hours. Stories are told of children who were made to get up at dawn to ply their books, whereas nowadays children are still in bed at six-thirty. How about that? Studies, it would appear, are deteriorating, and these people with newfangled ideas, these fresh air fiends come and tell us that our children study too hard.

There is a person called Demarquette, either a lunatic or a very wicked man, who professes to believe that it is good for one to run about naked in the sun. If he is not arrested, what are gaols built for? He is one of the men at the head of the boy-scout movement and gets his strange ideas from England, where he has lived and probably lost his mind. Now it is all right for boys to go to Meudon or Saint-Cloud on Sundays, and march singing through the woods with staffs on their shoulders, but their parents are anxious about that algebra problem which has to be turned in on Monday morning. And what if little Jean flunks at the end of the year and is made to take the whole course all over again? How dreadful! Madame Simonin is not averse to fresh air in reasonable quantities, but she doesn't want that little Cohen boy to get ahead of her son and grab the first prize in French composition as he did last year. So little Simonin stays at home and mumbles a tirade from *Le Cid* until he has mastered it, then he turns his attention to Dido's speech in the *Aeneid,* after which, with a bursting head, he takes a whack at German history and learns how to disentangle the various Electors of Brandenburg. No woods and sleeping under tents for him, but laurel wreaths on the twelfth of July.

This is 1912 and I suppose a fourteen-year-old French boy can look at the future as confidently as any boy in the world. His little brain is fast developing and will stand him in good stead when the time comes to make his mark. Already, his parents are choosing a profession for their son whose taste they try to direct. A tutor comes to coach him if he is backward. He has so much to learn, so many books to read if he is to keep abreast of little Cohen! And then professors are so exacting. And parents want their boys to carry off as many prizes as possible, prizes in Mathematics, in French Composition, in Latin, in Greek, in German, in English, any prize at any price, except the Gymnastics prize which is given with a smile and named last.

And so, little Jean, Gaston and Louis are doing very well in their studies and give fair enough promise of becoming capable engineers some day, or lawyers, or business men. Impossible is not French, they say. So thinks the French boy and so his parents. But they little know what a strange fate he is growing up to meet; they seldom if ever think of the new generation growing up on the other side of the Rhine, sturdy fellows whose bodies are carefully trained. The day is no longer very far when Jean will have to leave his books and be hustled off to the Belgian border to fight those fellows back, if he can. I wonder if he will be ready.

PART TWO

CHAPTER ONE

Both at home and at school, we would often hear the Balkan War mentioned and sometimes discussed, but I need hardly say that my ideas on the subject were hazy and my information uncertain. Friends of ours rejoiced over the Turkish defeats of Scutari and Janina and called their dogs Tari and Nina in honor of these events. There were a few people who sided with the Turks, one of them being the writer Pierre Loti who published a book called *La Turquie Agonisante* (Turkey on her Death-bed); the cover of this book bore a terrible and unforgettable photograph of a Turkish officer whose ears, nose and lips had been cut off by Serbian soldiers. I tried not to look at this book which was displayed in a store window, not far from our house, but of course I did and regretted it, because it interfered with my peace of mind when I had to go to bed and put out the light.

My mother was all for the Allies. "The Cross against the Crescent," she said. So thought the rector of the American Church, who created a sensation by saying from the pulpit that he hoped the Almighty would everlastingly

113

punish the Turk; this feeling he expressed in four short words which gave the congregation a jolt and were long remembered. My father, who knew Constantinople and had friendly dealings with the Turks, did not share this hatred of the fez. In fact, he wore a fez himself, at home, but I am getting off the track.

No one seemed to think that anything would come of this war which was really the beginning of Europe's downfall. It was considered a rather good thing that the sick man of Europe, as Turkey was called, should be pushed off the Continent where he retained only a foothold, and that the Balkan people should win their independence. A few intellectuals bemoaned the fate of Turkey and brought to mind the fact that she had been France's ally in the days of Francis the First; moreover, they pointed out that her conquerors would soon be wrangling among themselves and keep Europe in a dangerous state of fermentation. All of this was, of course, absolutely true, but no one, need I say, heeded these prophetic words. It was more amusing to joke about the whole thing as was done in a music-hall show called *Madame est Serbie!*

Just about this time, the tango came into fashion and somehow it seemed to dispel any sad thoughts brought on by the slaughter in distant Serbia. I knew from certain hushed whispers and horrified raising of eyebrows that the tango was supposed to be a naughty dance. Decent people

114

frowned on it and old Pope Pius the Tenth was so pained
by its growing success that he tried to have another dance
introduced to take its place, the prim Venetian *Furlana*,
which one danced at a distance of two or three feet from
one's partner, preferably with a *fazzoletto* or handkerchief
in one's hand. Parisians looked on and grinned, their faith
in tango unperturbed.

In those days, my sister Retta took piano lessons from
a black-eyed lady by the name of Madame de Las Palmas.
As I remember her, this lady wore a slight moustache
and smelt faintly like a zoo, but her rendering of Sinding's
Frühling was, to a certain extent, a sort of compensation.
Anyhow she taught my sister to play Clementi correctly
and to this day I can listen to that gentleman's simple
tunes with pleasure, because they bring up so many
memories of happy days.

It is a terrible leap from Clementi to tango, but Retta
was unafraid. One afternoon she came home with an album
which she had purchased with her monthly allowance.
On the cover was a picture of a *gaucho* with full lips and
half-closed eyes dancing with an equally exotic looking
lady. My sister went to the piano, opened her album with
a firm hand and began to play. Her face wore a frown and
the tip of her tongue stuck out between her teeth. I don't
think she could have been more than fifteen, as her hair
was still down her back, and she played as only a young

girl can play who has studied Clementi; there was nothing languorous about her touch, it was bold and firm, and as straightforward as she was herself; in fact, I have never known anyone who missed the point of tango with such utter innocence, but she was determined to learn this music, and learn it she did.

My mother, who had no ear at all and could hardly tell a hymn from the Star Spangled Banner, was probably unaware of her daughter's doings and would have cared very little had she known that *Dans tes Bras* was being performed on our piano instead of the *Sonatine pour délier les doigts*. She was far too kind and liberal-minded to suspect evil where no evil was, and so Retta was allowed to forge ahead unhampered and unvexed. There came a day when she finally mastered two or three South American pieces and I can still see her intent expression as she played, her vigorous little hands patiently striking the keyboard, making the brass candlesticks quiver and jingle. I don't know what Madame de Las Palmas thought of this. Doubtless she was not informed.

By 1913, everyone was dancing the tango in some form or other. Mothers looked on as their daughters were instructed at Baraduc's dancing school where Mr. Washington Lopp gave a *comme il faut* version of the new step. Another dance made its appearance at this time, but it failed to make a hit, partly because it was believed to be

116

of German origin. The tune, unless I am mistaken, was called *La Très-Moutarde* (Too much Mustard).

Germany and the Germans were anything but popular at this time, neither did the Kaiser's visit to Agadir and the speech he delivered there do anything to mend matters. Small but significant incidents might have given the people of France an inkling of what was developing, straws in the wind which only the very wise observed with proper care. An Alsatian schoolmaster was prosecuted for anti-German sentiments. One of the Reich's military dirigibles flew over the fortified region of eastern France — by mistake, of course — and landed at Lunéville. Yet, a Franco-German war seemed of all things in the world the most improbable. In the history book which we studied at school, there was, concerning this matter, one sentence which I remember well because my mind reverted to it very often at a later period; it said that "wars were being gradually eliminated from the modern world" and that "nations would find it henceforth more profitable to settle their disputes peacefully at the Hague, where an International Court of Justice had been set up for that purpose (with the Kaiser's approval)."

Of course, I was too young to read the papers and knew practically nothing of what was going on in the world. Yet I remember that, one evening in August, 1911, my father and some friends of his were sitting in the garden,

117

drinking juleps, when the name of Agadir was mentioned. It had a strange sound and I listened. Some words were spoken which I have forgotten, then my father turned to a young Frenchman whose name was Hébrard, asking him what he thought of the situation. "I think," said Hébrard, "that we had better grease our bayonets."

There was something so sinister about this sentence that I cast it about in my mind for several hours. I had seen bayonets glittering in the sun at military parades and instinctively hated them. On the other hand, war meant excitement and no young boy was ever depressed by the prospect of excitement. So, with mixed feelings, I asked my mother if France and Germany were going to have another war. "Your father does not think so," she said, "and he is always marvelously well informed on politics."

I was at once relieved and a little disappointed. We lived in such dull times! Nothing ever seemed to happen, whereas other periods of French history seemed full of extraordinary events, and even though I disliked bayonets I loved history, little realizing that the bayonet is the pen with which history is written, and written in blood.

The last week in July 1914 is one which I can vividly recall. A few months before, my parents had decided to give up our Paris flat and to live in the neighborhood of Saint Germain en Laye, about forty-five minutes from Paris in the train. My father had rented a large and comfortable house surrounded by a lovely garden, and in this garden we were sitting and having tea on July 29, when someone came up to us with a paper in his hand. Who it was, I do not remember, but I do remember that the headlines of the paper were unusually large, and my mother said: "Oh, it isn't possible!" "Of course not," said my father quietly, "nobody wants war. To begin with, the German socialists would not allow it."

He sat in his light gray suit and white waistcoat, smoking a long Russian cigarette and looking so calm that we felt that everything was all right. The elms above our heads moved faintly in the breeze and wasps flew around the pot of honey on the table. How could anything be wrong, how could anything change, when all was as usual around us? I could not understand why my mother had looked so upset.

A few days went by and war was declared. On that fateful second of August, I ran up to my room and in a fit of patriotic ardor tore my German grammar in pieces, hoping to be rid of that hideous book forever. Maps were bought to follow the military operations, with little flags of different colors which one was supposed to place over the names mentioned in the communiqués. At first it was tremendously exciting, because the French armies crossed the German border almost immediately, in the lower part of Alsace, but when the enemy began sweeping down the French coal district, I soon found it dispiriting to pin the small tricolor flags farther and farther south every afternoon, and so gave up that occupation.

Our garden adjoined the main road from Paris to Saint Germain and from our windows we could see the troops marching away to battle in their murderous red trousers and dark blue coats, a nineteenth century uniform which made them living targets for the German guns. The soldiers sang lustily and moved briskly on in spite of the heat and their heavy packs. It was plain that these men were eager to fight and that their faith in France was intense. I watched them with a pounding heart as they went by waving their hands at us and shouting *Sur la Route de Louviers,* a gay, bawdy song which has cheered the souls of millions of young Frenchmen. Women of the village and their children walked alongside the soldiers, sometimes breaking into a run to keep up with them, handed them flowers or cigarettes, or bottles of wine. Most of these women were very brave and endeavored to laugh, but one covered her face with her blue apron and howled with grief. "Don't cry, *la petite mère*," said the men with their flat Parisian accent, "we'll come back." Not very many did, however.

I was then not quite fourteen and could not very well grasp the importance of what was going on. It seemed un-believable that the French armies should be retreating, because everybody knew that the German Emperor was a criminal, and I like all children instinctively believed history to be moral. How then could the Germans not be beaten, seeing that they were wrong and fighting an unfair war? One afternoon, my mother walked quickly into my room and opened a large wardrobe where our linen was kept. The servants brought in the wicker trunk and my mother began throwing sheets and towels into it. To see her filling the trunk in midsummer was strange enough, but that she should be doing it with such precipitation made it very alarming, and I asked her what was the matter.

"The Germans are coming," was all she answered, and sent me downstairs to help my sisters wrap the silver in paper.

In a few hours, our most valuable or necessary belongings had been put in trunks and we left the house, not without having carefully locked the door on which my father stuck a piece of paper advising any possible intruder that this was American property; above this document, my mother placed a small American flag, in the hope that it might deter the invader! This done, we drove to the station.

My father's intention was to take us to Paris, there to wait and see what would happen. This plan, to most of his friends, seemed like madness, as apparently nothing was able to stop the enemy and the Government itself had fled to Bordeaux, but my father was a confirmed optimist; he refused to believe that Paris could be taken and insisted that the German advance would be halted before it reached the capital. It appeared, when we arrived in Paris, that very few people shared this hopeful view of the situation, as the streets were empty and most of the houses had their shutters closed. Of course, a great many Parisians were spending their holidays in the country when the war broke out and did not find it necessary to come back. Those who were left were, as usual, the poor who had no means of getting away and a certain number of stubborn shopkeepers who had refused to be panic-stricken.

There were no taxis to be found, all these vehicles, as is well known, having been commandeered to carry the Paris garrison to the Marne where the battle was being fought. However, my father managed to secure a handcart on which he piled our luggage. All this I thought very exciting, particularly as I didn't have to push the cart through the streets; that was my father's task which he performed while we drove away in a horse cab.

Having crossed the Champs-Elysées and jogged up the heights of the Trocadéro, our cab took us right into the heart of our beloved Passy, where my father had secured some rooms, the day before, in an old fashioned pension, the Pension Mouton, at number 43 rue de la Tour.

CHAPTER TWO

In a novel I wrote some years ago, I described the Pension Mouton as accurately as I could, because I think that places of the type are so fast disappearing that some record of them should be made. As a matter of fact, the Pension Mouton no longer exists, having been torn down at the time the avenue Mozart was extended under the name of avenue du Président Doumer. Many old houses which stood in the way had to go, and with them our pension.

It was a dingy, Louis-Philippe house with a small front which proved deceptive, there being far more rooms at the back of it than the windows seemed to indicate from the street. This was due to the fact that the level of the street was much higher than the level of the garden behind the house. Once you were inside the building, a steep and narrow staircase covered with patched up carpet took you up to your room, if you wanted to rest, whereas an equally steep, narrow and shabby staircase took you down to the dining room in the basement, where you might obtain food provided you asked for it at the right time.

I was given a room with a red plush armchair and a brass bed, a mirror in a bamboo frame and an engraving of Murillo's Young Beggars. Looking out of the window, I saw a long and rather somber yard, which was really a portion of an alley of plane trees, cut off by a wall at a certain distance from the house. Neither grass nor flowers were to be seen in this so-called garden (*beau jardin ombragé* said a sign over the door of the pension), only a few hens scratching the ground or walking about aimlessly.

Meals were served in a long room with bare walls and no furniture except a table and chairs of the simplest description. A not very clean white cloth covered the table and two decanters were placed at each end, one containing red wine which tasted like ink and the other, white wine which might have been mistaken for vinegar, but my mother said we were not to complain of anything and that this was war.

I had no thought of complaining, however, being delighted with the idea that we were living through days which would go down in books as the most fateful in French history. And to be in a city which hundreds of thousands of German soldiers expected to enter within the next week . . . It gave one a feeling of pride to be there and not hiding away in some distant part of the provinces. The only people who seemed to be left in Passy were the janitors. Concierges are much laughed at in Paris, but they are always left to face the German army with no other weapons than a broom and a feather duster. The reason is, of course, that come what may, they have to keep guard in their *loges* and cannot desert their posts without losing their envied position forever. And so they stand, like the Roman soldier in Pompeii. They are an arrogant, bad tempered, inquisitive lot in general, although I know a few exceptions, but they are brave.

We had the whole Pension Mouton to ourselves, waiting for the news to get a little better, whereas it got steadily worse. However, my mother had such faith in my father's judgment that leaving the city was not even considered. There were very alarming rumors of *Uhlanen* or lancers having been seen in the forest of Saint Germain, and refugees from the provinces occupied by the enemy poured into Paris. Then one day, war was brought much closer to us in the shape of a bomb dropped by a German "Taube" airplane at the bottom of the avenue de l' Alma where it killed an old gentleman and a little girl. It was a Sunday morning and we were in the American Church, only two or three hundred yards away; the preacher had just ascended the pulpit and was about to begin his sermon when this ominous noise was heard. I do not remember that anyone left the church or showed any signs of excitement: German bombs were small in those days.

The weather being particularly fine, our parents took us

that afternoon to the Bois de Boulogne, where rows of trees had been hastily cut down and heaped across one of the main roads leading out of the city; *chevaux-de-frise* had been placed in front of these obstacles which, we were told, would retard the enemy if not stop him. All this seemed pitifully inadequate, even to me, and I realize what the French mean when they say that the nineteenth century ended in 1914. In 1914, the nineteenth century in blue coats and red trousers was trying to fight back our lovely twentieth century with its mud-colored uniforms and up-to-date methods of killing. I must add, however, to go back to my description, that a long trench had been dug on one side of the barricade, but it proved of very small comfort to Parisians who viewed it with a skeptical eye.

Several days went by, morning and evening bringing news of a retreat which looked more and more like a rout, in spite of the General Staff's efforts to disguise the terrible truth. Then, one morning in early September, the papers printed something which placed the same word on everybody's lips: a miracle. Somehow the overwhelming force of the German army had been stemmed; one of the Kaiser's generals had blundered and his army was separated from the rest of the main force. For a whole week the battle raged on the Marne and the German High Command, who characteristically set the precise hour of their entry into the capital of France, had to call off the party and draw

126

back under the withering fire of the *soixante-quinze* guns. All this, they said, was done *plangemäss,* that is, according to plan.

Parisians were so overjoyed that they seemed for a moment to have lost that critical sense which is one of their best qualities. It was said everywhere that the beginning of the end was in sight. My mother cried one minute and laughed the other. Only then did we realize how badly we had been frightened; my father was not ashamed of confessing that he had spent several nights wide awake and terribly worried.

By the 15th of September, the French armies being well entrenched at a comfortable distance from Paris, people began coming back to the city. They were sun-tanned and a little shamefaced, but their shame wore off as quickly as their tan and very few days passed before they were holding forth like everyone else, in that semi-heroic vein with which two wars have made us familiar. Mourning, however, was being seen more and more frequently in the streets and the first mood of enthusiasm changed quickly to one of sober determination.

What with refugees coming to our city for protection and what with Parisians returning to their homes, the capital's population soon exceeded its normal size. All available flats were quickly rented and not a hotel room was to be found anywhere. In spite of difficulties, however, and a certain amount of discomfort, optimism prevailed during the first few weeks which followed what was now called the Victory of the Marne. It was commonly thought that the war would be over by Christmas, and Christmas was only three months away. Great hopes were placed in the Russian armies which were vividly pictured as sweeping down through the plains of East Prussia; they were usually compared in newspapers to a gigantic steamroller crushing everything in its way. *Le rouleau compresseur russe* seemed a formidable ally to us and we looked into the future with absolute confidence. Of course, there were a few people who shook their heads lugubriously over their papers and spoke of a long war, a shortage of coal and food restrictions, but they were frowned upon if not publicly insulted.

Before the month was out, we had returned to our house in the country, which we found exactly as we had left it, peaceful and undisturbed, with the elms and the horse-chestnuts in the garden turning to gold. As I look back on those days which seem to have been made even more distant by the crowded events of the last three years, I sometimes wonder if they belong to my life or if I am only remembering what has been told me about somebody else. I am not old; yet — and I believe that I share this feeling with a great many people of my generation — I cannot rid myself of the idea that I have lived much longer than forty years and that our method of reckoning time is at fault. Multiplicity of events rather than length of days creates this impression of longevity ánd not a few among us might truly say with Baudelaire that they have more memories than if they were a thousand years old.

Be that as it may, I cannot say that I was made unhappy by the war of 1914. To begin with, selfish as this may seem, we had no relatives at the front, so that we were spared a peculiarly painful form of anxiety. On the other hand, I, being just fourteen, could not fully realize the magnitude and horror of the whole thing. It takes a great deal to quell the joy of living in a child's heart and we were not even within hearing distance of the battle that was now being fought from trench to trench. At home, everything was as usual. Sometimes, a whole day would go by without any mention being made of the struggle that was shaking our world. To be sure, my parents were worried and unhappy, but their sadness did not affect my spirits very seriously. I could not imagine that anything could happen to us and, so long as we were together, all was well. Neither was I disturbed by the fact that ten French departments were under German rule, because it seemed no more possible to me that France could lose this war than that the sun could drop out of the sky.

All of us were not at home, however. My sister Eleanor, who was married to an Englishman and had settled in

Trieste, was compelled to leave that city at the opening of the war. She and her husband did not have time to take with them more than a jewel box, leaving their flat full of furniture and books in the hands of the Austrian authorities. They succeeded in boarding the last ship that left for Venice, and having reached Italy proceeded directly to Genoa, where they made their home; there they lived until June 1940 when they were obliged to leave hurriedly, much as they had left Austria twenty-six years before.

The first excitement of the war abated somewhat by October and Europe settled down for her first winter under arms. There was little action on the French front and the communiqués grew briefer. In almost every French home, a map with rows of tiny flags showed the respective positions of Allied and German armies. No one talked of anything but the war and great comfort was derived from adding up the nations that now opposed Germany in her wild dreams of world supremacy. Food restrictions were not yet enforced and casualty lists had so far not been very heavy. Few people, if any, realized that we were plunging into a night of horror that was to darken the whole Continent for four years, but it is just as well that we do not know what is in store for us. As a child I used to wonder how it was that, being gifted with the power to see in all directions in the physical world, we could see only back of us and never ahead when it came to looking into time. This

providential blindness allows humanity to go on without
sinking into despair.

The war had been a very great shock to my mother.
Two days after Christmas of that year, she died suddenly.
On the eve of her death, which nothing in the world could
allow us to foretell, my sister Retta was sitting on the sofa
in the living room. As she looked out of the window, she
saw some men on ladders, hanging the garden gate with
black draperies according to European custom when a
funeral is to take place. So dreadfully vivid was this scene
to her that she called Anne to witness it, but the latter
could see nothing but the empty garden in the bleak afternoon.

Although we now lived thirty-five miles from Paris, I still attended the Lycée Janson and had to get up at the crack of dawn to catch the train. My mother could wake me up simply by standing at the foot of my bed and calling to me ever so softly; even as I slept, something in me recognized her presence and I invariably responded. But no child loved his bed on a cold morning more deeply than I did, and getting up was an awful struggle.

"Come on now," my mother would say, "come on."

She half whispered these words; there was nothing harsh in her voice or in her face as she stood by me, holding a candle which lit up her beautiful gray eyes. A quarter of a century seems not to have effaced a single detail of this moment of my life. The stillness of the house and of the garden outside, the dark rooms in which the candle-light shone like a star, my mother's footsteps, so light that they seemed a part of silence, all comes back to me with amazing precision.

When the Christmas holidays were over, that year, it

132

was my sister Retta who took my mother's place, woke me up and made my tea while I dressed with a heavy heart. As I ate my breakfast, she watched me with her big, tragic eyes which filled with tears from time to time. Neither one of us could speak.

Having closed the gate behind me, I would run to the station down the silent road, with the stars still bright in the sky. How the books rattled in my knapsack as I hurried along the sidewalk! I never missed the six forty-five train and always secured a seat by the window. The second class coach with its windows tightly closed smelled terribly, but one soon got accustomed to it, I found, and the warmth was delightful. Most of the people in the coach nodded over their newspapers or talked in low murmurs of hard times and the war, while I plunged into a book and thus escaped from the world around me.

One of the many stories I read in this way was Chateaubriand's *Atala,* a book which I dread to reread for fear I might be disillusioned about it. Somehow it has become fixed in my mind as a thing of unsurpassed beauty, a sort of dream from which it would be stupid to awake unless one had to. Oh, it mattered very little whether the coach smelled of stale tobacco smoke and people spat in a horrible way! I was on the banks of the Mississippi River with René, watching the floating islands as the Father of Waters bore them gently seaward with their exotic vegetation and

133

strangely colored birds. I was listening to Chactas the Indian as he held forth by the flickering light of a camp fire, and with hot, silly tears rolling down my cheeks, I buried lovely Atala in the gloom of an American cave. The flowery beauty of Chateaubriand's style enraptured me like the strains of some unearthly music. I felt, no doubt, like the readers of 1802 when this fanciful picture of the New World was placed before their eyes: my critical sense was weak but my imagination proved ready to follow the French Vicomte wherever he wished to take me.

I stayed at school all day and returned home by the evening train. What this meant can hardly be realized except by children who are, as I was, passionately attached to the place they live in. To me, the lycée was no less than a gaol and I developed a real loathing for its dingy brown walls. As I sat in the dark classroom, I thought with an almost morbid longing of the snow falling in the country and of my sisters looking at the white garden from the drawing-room windows; and I could not rid myself of the strange idea that my mother was still at home, sitting by a window with a book in her hand, or lying asleep in a big armchair with a long gray shawl wrapped around her shoulders.

As the casualties at the front became heavier the Paris hospitals soon filled up and it was decided that some wounded soldiers would be cared for in the larger schools, where accommodations could be found. Over one hundred were sent to Janson and lodged in the rooms on the second floor, just above the classrooms. War was thus brought exceedingly close to us; it still sends a pang through my heart to think of the dreadful groans of pain we often heard during class hours. When the wounded were strong enough they were taken out walking by their nurses in the yard, and I shall never forget the impression which these maimed and unhappy looking men made upon me as they limped about in their pale blue uniforms.

As I have already said, I stayed at school all day, being what is called a *demi-pensionnaire*. After classes, the "free" boys went home, leaving pensionnaires and demi-pensionnaires to an extra hour of work before lunch. I studied, mainly to get away from myself and to try to conquer a heaviness of heart which made a trial of every hour. Thus I soon acquired a taste for learning and gradually made up for years of laziness. There was, I discovered, something fascinating in making your own what you found in books, a chapter of French history or even a theorem, anything you could really master and absorb. I felt a growing desire to know all there was to know under the face of the sun and ingenuously believed that by dint of perseverance I should some day gratify this monstrous wish.

Gloom prevailed around us. It was heavily impressed on us by our professors that thousands of men were dying in Flanders and in Champagne so that we might live and study in peace. Moreover, it was impossible to forget the presence of the wounded soldiers on the floor above, and several boys already were in mourning for their fathers or brothers.

Of course, patriotism was deemed a cardinal virtue in those days, but it was patriotism of a somber quality and mixed with barely concealed anguish. In my class, the boys were wondering whether they would ever be given a chance to enlist. Among the most impatient was a fellow called Durieu. I seldom spoke to him, yet I liked him. He was gay and boisterous, with something about him which might have reminded me of Steerforth, had I read *David Copperfield*. His pleasing, cheerful face still haunts me from time to time and I don't think I shall ever forget his clear, ringing laughter. Though our elder by a few months, he was barely over sixteen when it was whispered in the classroom that Durieu had decided to run away from home and join the army. A collection was taken up to enable him to buy a railroad ticket and against my better judgment I gave what we all gave, one franc. It was preposterous for a lad of sixteen to go to the front without his parents' consent, and sure enough he came back about ten days later, having been sent home to his distracted mother by the gendarmes. However, he had read too much about Barra and Viala, the drummer boys of the Revolution, and at the end of a few months he ran away again. This time, he succeeded in reaching the front and remaining there, and I don't think many weeks went by before he was killed.

That year, Anne and Retta joined the Red Cross and became nurses at the Hôtel Ritz which had been turned into a hospital. They were both very young and looked like angels in their white uniforms, but even then I thought it was a ghastly experience for persons of their age to have to face. However, they seemed to consider it quite natural and went about their work every day with thousands of unselfish women who gave up their time, their youth, and sometimes their lives without a murmur.

Those sinister days stamped me and many others far more deeply than might be imagined. Had I been younger, the impression left on my mind would have been slight. Had I been older, I might better have grasped the significance of what was going on at the front, but somehow fifteen was the wrong age for the experience we were living through, and the shock was bad. The communiqués which I now read attentively emphasized the fact that each square mile of territory that was wrested from the Germans in appalling battles of Champagne and Artois cost a great many lives. The dominant note in the streets of Paris was black and there was practically no family that did not have to go into mourning before the year 1915 was out. Nevertheless it was beginning to be realized by some that, in spite of initial victories, Germany was losing the war, just as she is losing the war today.

Most boys were more lighthearted than I, or seemed so, and played much as they might have done in normal times. However, I have often thought that one of the secrets of French character and French courage is to be found in an old Provençal proverb, which says: *"Le rire dans la rue, les pleurs à la maison."* In other words; laugh in the street and do your crying at home.

There were no more South Americans with us; they had all fled like frightened birds, and who could blame them? As a sort of compensation, we had a good many refugees from the occupied provinces and got along pretty well with them, although they were different from us in many ways, and to be different from the rest of the crowd is a dreadful sin in the eyes of a boy.

One of these refugees I remember very distinctly. His name was Bosse. He came from Noyon, in Picardie, where Calvin was born. No sooner had I clapped eye on Bosse than I was filled with a strong dislike of him and everything connected with him. He was a sturdy boy of sixteen, with red hair, a low forehead, a turned-up nose and a face covered with freckles. Now I come to think of it, there was

138

nothing wrong about him, except that he was uncommon-
ly plain, spoke with an ugly provincial accent and depended
too much on his physical strength to obtain what he
wanted. We spoke very little, he and I, but I secretly
prayed that the Allies might swiftly recapture Noyon, so
that Bosse could go home. I contrived never to sit next to
him in class and made efforts not to think of him, but he
was often at the back of my mind and whenever Noyon
was mentioned in the communiqués, my heart pounded
heavily with a mixture of hope and dread. At last, after
many months of weary fighting, the news came that the
British had succeeded in occupying the town of Noyon, and
I fancied that Bosse would immediately pack his belongings and rid us of his presence. Nothing of the kind happened; he stayed on and on, that year and the next, and I
simply had to reconcile myself to the thought that he
would never go. Indeed, I left the *lycée* before he did.

I cannot say that, materially, we suffered much from the
war in 1915. Food was still plentiful and in spite of the
fact that all the great coal mines of the North were in German hands, it was possible to keep the houses reasonably
warm, thanks to importations from England. Neither
could Paris be truthfully called gloomy. Theaters and cafés
remained open and were usually crowded, every variety of
amusement being offered to the men who came from the

front on furlough. No matter what the feelings of individuals might be, a show of gaiety was made to keep up the spirit of the soldiers, and I don't suppose the streets of the capital had ever known such animation. The uniforms of seven or eight Allied nations brightened the boulevards where so much black was seen worn by civilians. Thus was a strange and indefinable atmosphere created, one of artificial cheerfulness struggling with a strong undercurrent of grief and anxiety. Optimism, however, was the only mood tolerated. Grumblers were silenced by hoots or cries of *"Embusqué!"* (Slacker) which cut very deep at the time. The *poilu* became a sort of idol, his uncouth appearance being a source of inspiration for newspaper draughtsmen and writers of patriotic songs. One enthusiastic author declared that the mud which they brought with them from the trenches was no less than sacred. A nickname was found for that redoubtable weapon, the bayonet; it was called Rosalie, and Rosalie was extolled to the skies. Such was the state of mind of Paris after twelve months of warfare.

By the end of 1915, our lease was near expiration and my father decided that we would return to Paris to live, as none of us really liked living in the country and it was inconvenient for him to have his home so far from his office. Flats, however, were very scarce in the city and it was a problem to find one big enough for all of us. The first weeks of 1916 went by and my father had not yet succeeded in his endeavors. Our furniture was now in storage at Bedel's, the most important storage company in Paris, and we were all back again at the Pension Mouton.

Our rooms were small and shabbily furnished in the plainest Louis-Philippe or, as the French disparagingly call it, Louis-Philippard manner. Yet we felt so happy to be back in Paris that we hardly noticed the broken down armchairs and threadbare rugs. This love of Paris was so deep in our hearts that words can no more express it than they can express the love of one human being for another. I delighted in the thought that I was a part of Paris and that Paris was a part of me. Like many others, to be sure I felt that this city belonged to me and that I had the right to be proud of it. The fact that I was American-born of American parents could in no way alter the equally indisputable fact that I was a Parisian.

So once more, we were having our meals in the long, bare dining room with the two decanters of sour wine placed symmetrically on the bespotted tablecloth. Far more people, however, sat at the table than in September 1914. The place of honor was given to an old baroness who had known better days and was ending her life in poverty and solitude, having no friends and no one to talk to now except the ever-changing inmates of the Pension Mouton.

She looked like an elderly sheep dressed in black lace and spoke in a mournful voice of her husband, General de B., who died some ten years before I was born. Next to her sat a middle-aged Mexican lady whose green sweater was outrageously and purposely tight, but whose tongue, by way of compensation, was loose; a heavy brown fringe fell over her eyes; she smoked cigarettes and talked about men in a manner which made the baroness wince.

An old gentleman named Dubuas presided over our meals, a tall, stiff, military looking person with a lantern jaw and a cold blue eye; breeding and an almost uncontrollably bad temper seemed to be perpetually at war within him, and it was plain that even when he was at his politest, he was at the same time longing to be rude. A flagon of brandy was placed in front of him with his coffee, but however liberally he helped himself to the former, it never appeared to affect him in the least, except that he became more and more dissatisfied with the conduct of the war. With his head thrown back, his legs crossed and one hand thrust in his waistcoat, he tore the Allied generals to pieces, railed at their plans and spoke darkly of the ultimate fate of Paris. We listened in horrified silence, realizing that something was wrong with the old gentleman's brain. Not being accustomed to this kind of language, I received a series of shocks from Mr. Dubuas' speeches and, with disgust in my heart, beheld my first defeatist.

Memories of Happy Days

There were other people too, a rather mysterious woman who wore handsome rings on dirty hands and discussed racy novels with the Mexican lady; a pharmacist, mobilized a few weeks before, who sadly and accurately predicted that he would soon be "eating vegetables by their roots"; an English lieutenant, also on leave of absence, who grinned mutely and looked at us all in an amused sort of way, as if he were having his meals in the monkey cage at the zoo; a shy little woman dressed in black who always appeared with red eyes and never spoke above a whisper, brushed the crumbs of bread into the palm of her hand at the end of each meal and ate them, as nuns are supposed to do. All these people, brought together by circumstances, separated after exchanging a few trite words, each going to his own fate, shrouded in his own little mystery. I watched them and wondered. There was something which I found very disturbing in the thought that they would probably disappear forever from my life, in a little while, and that I would never know what had become of them; so I tried to imagine how they spent their time, what misfortunes might come their way or in what manner they might achieve happiness and success. It irked me to believe that we knew so little about each other, that we lived, as it were, in the dark, and that whether we lived at all or died made very little difference to the mass of humanity. When I heard of hundreds of thousands of men being killed in a battle, for instance the battle of Verdun which was then being fought, I felt that we were all surrounded by something horrible and mysterious and that we were spared or crushed at random like insects on a road. Yet, in spite of this fear, there was in me the growing belief that each particular destiny followed its course to the end, and that chance did not exist. How these views could be reconciled, I did not know, neither could I clearly have stated what I felt, but I was beginning to realize what a puzzling and uncomfortable position is that of man in his little world.

Death was a fact which I refused to accept or try to understand. When I learned that the pharmacist had been killed, exactly as he had feared and predicted, I was as shocked as if he had been a relative, because I had eaten two meals with him and he had asked me what I studied at school; I could not imagine him lying on the ground in his pale blue uniform, with his pince-nez shattered to pieces. Each time I heard of a friend of ours being killed, and this kind of news became more and more frequent, I received the same shock and tried desperately to comfort myself with the thought that it was perhaps not true, that there might have been a mistake. I struggled with all my might against the appalling facts which were darkening the life of almost every individual in the country to such a point that happiness seemed wiped out of our world forever.

Memories of Happy Days

There were gruesome tales of Belgian women and children being tortured by the enemy, of hostages being shot, in the north of France, after having been compelled to dig their own graves, and the sight of wounded soldiers in the streets was beginning to tell on sensitive people's nerves. The name of Verdun struck horror in every woman's breast. It looked as if we were sinking into a chaos of darkness, of mud and of blood, and so we reached the most sinister days of that black year, 1916.

CHAPTER FOUR

On a Thursday morning in March 1916, my father took me to the rue Cortambert where he had found and rented a flat large enough to contain us all. It was unfurnished and the rooms were absolutely bare, but no sooner had I stepped into the drawing room than I felt strangely and unaccountably happy, as if I had had a presentiment that better times were ahead. However, my father did not allow me to indulge in this prophetic mood very long and, handing me a yardstick and a piece of paper, told me that I was to measure the rooms and make as accurate a plan of the apartment as I could, so that we should know exactly where each piece of furniture was to go before we moved in.

Being rather deft with a pencil, I acquitted myself of my task fairly well, and two weeks later we had left the Pension Mouton forever. What trouble it meant to move in those days, with most of the men at the front and none but a few white haired *déménageurs* left, is difficult to im-

146

agine now, but we were all so eager to help that, short of hoisting the piano up the staircase, we did practically everything. Fortunately, the flat was on the second floor, or to be more precise, on that confusing floor called the *entresol* and invariably mixed up with the third floor. From the front windows, we could see the Protestant Chapel, inside of which I had, years before, sat on my father's hat, and by leaning out ever so little it was possible to catch a glimpse of the people walking under the horse chestnut trees of the avenue Henri Martin. The back rooms looked out on a court with a lonely palm tree in the middle; these rooms were a bit dark, but we were delighted with everything and refused to go to bed, that evening, before every piece of furniture had found its place as indicated by my sketch.

In spite of our zeal, however, it took us no less than a week to make the house look like home. We were overjoyed at the results, being, like a great many young people, immensely proud of every stick of furniture we owned. The three front rooms opened into each other, thus producing an effective enfilade which, I insisted, reminded one of Versailles. As a matter of fact, our window curtains were far from new and had faded; also, our Savannah furniture was in urgent need of upholstering, but we were not very critical.

Nevertheless, there was something wrong with the

147

house, and that we soon found out: it was not heated. My father knew it, of course, when he signed the lease, but he thought that with wood fires and particularly with our *salamandre*, we would not do so badly. A *salamandre*, I must explain, is a coal stove with little panes of isenglass through which one can watch the coal being consumed. There is hardly a house in France without a *salamandre*, at least there was not in those days; its place is usually under the dining-room mantelpiece so that it obstructs the fireplace. When properly attended to, it gives a reasonable amount of heat, but more often than not exhales a mephitic odor of carbonic gas, in spite of which it has remained popular during many decades.

So we counted on our *salamandre* to help us through the freezing months of early spring, but coal was so scarce and the *salamandre* consumed so much that we had to be content with a meager log fire around which we huddled in our overcoats. March and April can be very bitter in Paris, and it soon became so difficult to find even wood that we resorted to the old trick of burning paper balls in a grate; but a paper fire can't be kept up very long and there was not an abundance of paper. So we froze. One day, however, one of my sisters came home with a basket full of coal which she had bought at a reasonable price from a woman in the street. Paper and kindling wood were placed in a grate and the coal arranged on top as carefully

148

as peaches in a fruit dish. Then a match was applied and we all looked on cheerfully, but the fire went out almost immediately for the simple reason that the coal was nothing but lumps of ice covered with coal dust.

Food was rationed, of course. We always rose from the dining-room table feeling hungry, but the hope that these restrictions were helping the country win the war made them a little easier to bear. Much comfort was derived by some from making fun of the German war bread, called KK bread. Neutral travelers coming back from Germany through Denmark or Holland told ghastly stories of what they had seen among our enemies, but the plight of the German people aroused little pity on our side of the Rhine: it was felt that they could end the war by rising against their demented leaders who were sending them by hundreds of thousands to a perfectly useless death.

By the middle of 1916, we were all so thoroughly accustomed to war conditions that they seemed quite normal and peacetime conditions a sort of foolish dream. War was accepted by an immense majority and grumblers or defeatists were publicly upbraided when they were not simply sent to gaol. The walls of Paris were covered with posters advocating loans to the Government. Some of these posters, the work of local celebrities such as Abel Faivre, Cappiello, Simon and Albert Guillaume, expressed almost every mood from irony to heroic wrath. The German soldier was

seen gnashing his teeth at the Gallic rooster coming out
of its twenty franc gold piece. French infantrymen wearily
trudging through Flanders mud with a blood red sky reflected in every puddle so that the soldiers appeared to be
walking through gore, such was the theme of another poster with which Parisians were confronted at all hours of
the day. Later on, when signs of Germany's exhaustion
began to show, a new poster urged every Frenchman to
give some money "for the last fifteen minutes," "*pour le
dernier quart d'heure,*" but the dernier quart d'heure was
a very long time in coming to an end and the draughtsmen I have mentioned had to tax their imagination as
never before to induce people who had given a great deal to
give even more.

The war had become a sort of *idée fixe* with everybody
and it seemed impossible to escape from this obsession.
No other subject could be mentioned, no book written that
did not deal with the only topic readers were interested in:
when and how Germany was going to be beaten. Two
communiqués were issued daily, one at five A.M., the other
at three P.M. Each was analysed and discussed with the
help of maps and tiny flags or, failing these, with bits of
matches and lines drawn across tablecloths, to the point
that one part of France seemed to be fighting the war and
the other explaining it. Cafés and drawing rooms were
filled with amateur strategists who exchanged their views

so passionately that *l'union sacrée* was more than once forgotten. Rumors, canards of all descriptions found ready listeners everywhere. At last, a reaction set in. Ladies in knitting circles, who could not meet without asking each other if they had read the communiqué, finally agreed that the war was not to be mentioned while they worked and that delinquents would be fined. Fun was poked at parlor generals who suggested what they would do if they were at the head of the Allied armies.

Meanwhile, most of France's youth was being horribly slaughtered on the battlefields of Champagne and Argonne, and with the help of enemy propaganda, discouragement began to creep in like poison in the veins of an exhausted man. Clandestinely printed pamphlets somehow found their way into people's hands. It was whispered that the Allies would never succeed in thrusting the German armies out of France and that the country was slowly bleeding to death. The high water mark of defeatism was not reached, however, until 1917 when old Clemenceau arraigned a group of traitors and had them shot, thus virtually winning the war for France. But before that the civilian morale fell extremely low. A cartoon came out in *Le Journal* summing up the situation in a few pencil strokes and four words. Two soldiers were seen in a trench, gloomily shaking their heads over a Paris paper while one said: *"Pourvu qu'ils tiennent!"* (Let's hope they hold out!)

Monotony was the keynote of those unforgettable years, monotony in death and horror. To be sent to the front and to come back alive seemed almost miraculous. Leaves of absence so long and earnestly wished for were fraught with anxiety. "Is this the last time I shall see him? Will he come back to me again?" were questions too plainly read in the eyes of women who walked arm in arm with *permissionaires*. Each one of these women was France all by herself, as it were, a tortured and courageous France with tragedy in her eyes and a smile on her lips. How self-sacrificing these women were for four long and harrowing years is apt to be forgotten now, because their unhappy country has been crushed and little real sympathy ever goes to the conquered, but I cannot believe that all this sorrow has been in vain and that the hour of compensation will not strike, some day, for the martyred French nation.

Paris is usually thought of as a city of pleasure, and it is that, or was, but like most great cities it is a world in itself and, as such, a great religious center. Foreigners are apt to overlook this fact. Their conception of the Parisian as a light-headed and sensual being is only partly true. The war or any great national danger brings out a natural piety in the Parisian, the result of many centuries of Christian belief. From 1914 to 1918, very few churches in Paris remained empty. On week days as well as on Sundays, crowds were to be seen kneeling in deep silence at the foot

152

of the altars. I mention this in order that the hasty sketch I give here may be complete and that the whole of the picture may not be taken up by the Boulevards and their frivolous activity. To be sure, relief from anxiety was sought by most in various forms of pleasure, but the Church exerted a powerful attraction on thousands of men and women bewildered by the terrific struggle that was rending the Continent in two.

At school, I found a means of escape from a confusing world in my studies. The war, however, was as present there as elsewhere. Each important piece of news was written out in large letters on our blackboard by the more patriotic among us and stared us in the face during class hours. Contrary to my expectations in 1914, German was still taught and I cannot remember that the attendance was greater for English than for the language of our enemies. I may add that the British were immensely popular in Paris and that the Entente Cordiale was a reality which even the Germans were compelled to admit.

We were not many at home. My sister Eleanor was living in Genoa with her husband. Mary, whose health was precarious, lived in Rome, and Lucy, who was also delicate and could not stand war conditions in France, was sent to Virginia where she spent over a year with our relatives in that state.

Once a week, Anne and Retta had dinner with us and

it was my business to see them back to the Ritz by ten o'clock. I vividly remember those trips through the darkened streets of Paris, the eerie look of the rue de Rivoli with its empty arcades and the black silhouette of an occasional policeman in the dim, bluish light, as well as the loud, reverberating noise our footsteps made in the deserted squares.

Sometimes, I went to see my sisters in the daytime, but I invariably came away with a feeling of inexpressible sadness. In spite of the fact that the Ritz was now a hospital, it still retained a sort of horrible glamour, still looked like what it had been formerly: one of the smartest hotels in the world. One could hardly realize that behind the white doors in the long passages, wounded men were struggling for their lives and that an enormous amount of suffering and misery was harbored in a building whose very name spelled easy living. The cheerfulness of the nurses was obviously put on; it was a part they played with all the courage they were able to muster. One had to smile in the face of death, otherwise it meant defeat. We all understood that, but no one lived up to that principle more consistently than the women in the hospitals, and it may well be said that the war was partly won by their unflinching sense of duty.

The months dragged on wearily and the end was far from near when we plunged into our third war winter. I

154

don't think I am exaggerating when I say that almost everyone shivered and starved through December, January, February and March. It was then that a modern form of an old pestilence broke out suddenly and took us back to the days of the Black Death. Many thousands of civilians died of the Spanish flu. In a few days, sometimes in a few hours, they passed from this world into the next with blackened, unrecognizable faces.

Probably the lack of coal was more keenly felt even than the lack of food, but the combination of the two helped the new disease to spread and greatly jeopardized the future of the race. The schools were heated and so were most public buildings; very little could be done, however, about heating apartment houses and I have not yet forgotten certain bleak, icy days in December when I sat in my overcoat, at home, and blew on my fingers as I tried to learn my lessons in spite of the temperature. It was a strange experience, living through those years with the feeling that the war could not be lost and yet that the tide might turn against us at any moment. Many felt that only by a series of miracles had the German armies been held off. Less mystical minded people contended that the *soixante-quinze* guns were to be credited with keeping the enemy at bay, but it was something far more human than the seventy-five millimeter gun; it was a desperate determination not to die. The story was told of a French

155

soldier clambering out of a trench to meet the enemy; seeing that he was practically alone in coming out, he turned around and realized that almost all the men with him had been wiped out and were lying dead or dying in the trench. He then uttered a strange and magnificent cry which soon became known all over the country and stirred the whole nation to a new pitch of enthusiasm:

Debout les morts!

As I write these words today, I feel that no German victory can ever efface such memories from the minds of French men and women. It was heroism on an almost supernatural plane, something which German might was powerless to conquer, because this war was a test of spirit even more than a test of strength; it was a time when whole regiments believed that they saw Joan of Arc leading them in battle and when dead men were seen to rise and pick up their guns. Mass hallucinations are ever possible, but the fact that hallucinations such as these could occur — if they were hallucinations — is in itself a more interesting fact than the reality or the non-reality of what the soldiers believed they saw in the sky; it proved that France of all times, medieval and modern, was one and indivisible in the face of that perpetual threat to civilization: the German State.

America's entry into the war came, we all felt, in the nick of time to save the world from a major disaster. It certainly enabled the French to "hang on," *tenir*, as they said, and face more months of bitter fighting. I do not think the bulk of the nation will ever forget it.

On a morning in July 1917, I walked up the Boulevard
Saint-Michel as far as the Place de la Sorbonne and, with
a pounding heart, stepped inside the building where I was
to pass — or so I hoped — my *baccalauréat*. All I was
allowed to carry with me was a fountain pen, the paper
being furnished by sharp eyed *huissiers* who walked up
and down the examination room with creaking shoes.

I struggled through an apparently simple page of Livy,
which, I discovered on closer scrutiny, was one long series
of clever pitfalls. Having worried this specimen of Latin
prose into French, I had to worry a page of French into
something like Latin. And that was a morning's work.

After a hasty lunch nervously gulped down at a neighboring *bistro*, I went back to the examination room and
wrestled with an aphorism by Diderot which I had to explain, analyse and otherwise torment until I had enlarged
in about fifteen hundred words on a thought which he
had neatly expressed in twelve or fourteen. I did this with
a glib pen and handed in what I considered an excellent

piece of writing, but I feel sure that my face and ears would burn with shame if I were to read it today.

Next came the Physics and Chemistry test; the usual indiscreet questions were asked as to how certain acids behave when mixed in a glass, why apples fall from trees instead of shooting up to the zenith, and so forth. My answers were wild, if ingenious.

The following day was one which I had dreaded for a whole twelvemonth. Irascible professors, fingering penholders and wincing as if in pain at almost every answer they got, sounded the depths of our ignorance and sent us back to our seats in despair. The Physics professor played with me like a cat with a half-dead mouse. "What," he said holding his inkstand, "what would you suggest if I were to ask for the temperature of this object?" I was appalled, I still am, at the unfairness of such a question which was not even vaguely hinted at in our textbook. At any rate, I have learned that dipping a thermometer in the inkstand will not do, because my torturer looked at me and said: "For that answer alone, you deserve to be kicked all the way to the rue de la Sorbonne! However," he added, "I suppose you will pass on account of that French dissertation you handed in. Now go away!"

So I did pass after all, and went home singing to myself for sheer glee.

A week later, my father took me to his favorite tailor,

159

facetiously called Slaughter and Carver by the more fastidious among the British colony of Paris, and there I was
fitted out for a khaki uniform made of the finest cloth,
with big square pockets and shoulder straps. A cap with
an American eagle was added and I am frank to admit that
I fancied myself enormously in these martial clothes. Perhaps I should have explained that I was joining up with
the American Field Service. I was then almost seventeen
and it was considered proper that I should "do something"
since everybody else in the world seemed to be doing something for or against the Allies.

For the last month, I had been learning to drive a car
and had at last been awarded my license. The next step was
to be presented in my handsome uniform to Mr. Stephen
Gallatti who was then at the head of the American Field
Service in France. It happened that my father had known
Mr. Gallatti's father, which made it easier to wave aside
slight difficulties, my age, for instance. I was accepted and
booked to leave Paris by the end of the month for a training camp near Meaux. Mr. Gallatti was a man of few
words, but he spoke kindly to me and I need hardly say
how flattering to my vanity all this was, or how superior I
felt to my schoolmates who would be pursuing their studies
while I drove my ambulance at the front.

Our Paris headquarters were located in a very fine old
house in the rue Raynouard with a park which extended as
160

far as the quai de Billy (now known as the quai de Tokio). It was in this house that I first came in contact with a crowd of American boys. They were all a trifle older than I, and how different from the type of humanity I was accustomed to is well nigh impossible to convey. To be sure, I had been brought up in an American family and had met some of my parents' friends, but never before had I looked in the face of an American college man. Being absurdly shy at that age, I was tongue-tied when my new comrades asked me questions about myself. My French accent made me painfully self-conscious and, fearing that I should betray my uneasiness by blushing, I immediately proceeded to turn crimson, with the result that I was soon left alone. That irritated me because I wanted very much to mix with the crowd. I liked these men, although their ways did seem a little strange at first. There was something absolutely straight-forward and guileless about them which attracted me. Somehow, they weren't at all like French boys. Their laughter was almost childlike, their minds entirely free from those preoccupations which made people in Paris look so serious. One had the impression that they had come to Europe on some extraordinary holiday. For three years I had not heard men laugh and joke in this way and I felt at once pleased and a little bewildered.

On the 29th of July, we were assembled in the park where our brand new ambulances were waiting for us. I examined mine nervously. It was a Ford and I did not know how to drive a Ford, but I thought that I would manage somehow. We stood at attention and Mr. Gallatti made a short speech, then we hopped into our cars and off we drove: that is, off the others drove, one by one, through the majestic old gates. Unfortunately for me, there was also a majestic old stepping stone into which I ran for no other reason than uncontrollable excitement. I may as well say now that I did not drive well and that a Ford was to me like a vicious, untamed animal with a will of its own and intentions which I could not fathom. However, with the help of a grumpy mechanic, my Ford was in running order almost twenty minutes after the accident I have mentioned and I drove it cautiously through those gates. How mortified I was, can easily be imagined. One of the French mechanics who was attached to our ambulance section sat by me and watched my every move with considerable distrust. I don't remember how we ever got out of Paris and caught up with the other cars; it still seems a little miraculous to me.

Our training camp was at a place in the country called Moulins-de-Meaux. We slept on cots in a very large barn and ate at a tremendously long table on which we rapped with our tin plates, like babies, when the food was too long in coming. The rest of the time, we drove our Fords up and down the roads, for practice, learned how to turn them

162

around quickly, how to get out of ditches and, worst of all, how to start them on a hill. I did all this very badly. What happened to my Ford when I got behind the wheel was unthinkable. Walls seemed to rise suddenly out of the ground for me to crash into. When I thought I was doing well, I would see peasants throw up their arms on the road side as I passed them. One day, I whizzed by an army truck and my instructor, who was sitting by me, pulled out his handkerchief to mop his brow. "I guess we missed that truck by one inch," he remarked.

I don't think he really enjoyed my company. He was very patient, but I usually succeeded in making him lose his temper before the lesson was over, and the more he shrieked, the less I understood what he meant. One day, he was trying to make me back between two rows of sticks, not one of which did I miss. Some country girls watched this humiliating performance and nudged each other, which infuriated my instructor, who was twenty-five and sensitive. I suppose he was ashamed of me. "That one," he said in broken French as he pointed to me, "that one will *never* learn." He thought I could not understand. It was all very painful.

My comrades were as good a lot of men as I have ever seen anywhere. They were all university students and had come over for no other reason than an idealistic love of France and democracy. Although I felt a little diffident

163

about speaking to them at first, I soon grew to like them. Their gaiety and lightheartedness made me forget how homesick I was. I think that what struck me most in all these men was their sincerity. There was nothing at the back of their minds when they spoke; they were no angels, but they did not lie and they never said anything that could hurt one's feelings even though they did laugh at each other in a seemingly merciless way. I got on very well with all of them and I think they liked me. When I had explained that I was American, although I had never set foot in my country, they took it upon themselves to perfect my education by proving to me that America was better than any country in the world. I remember particularly a law student from New York city. There was a sort of emotional logic in his speeches when he spoke of America, and a look of immense pride in his large, intelligent brown eyes when he considered that I was properly convinced.

When we had all been trained to our instructor's satisfaction, we left Moulins-de-Meaux for a little town called Triaucourt, on the outskirts of the Forest of Argonne. Triaucourt was practically deserted; only the curé, the mayor and a few old peasants remained, and most of the houses were shuttered up until better times. We slept in our cars, which were lined up along the sidewalk of the Grand' Rue. How long we were to stay at Triaucourt, we were not told,

164

but time soon began to grow heavy on our hands and we longed to be sent to a more exciting place. There was a pretty old church to see and pleasant walks to take through the country, but my comrades insisted that they had not come all the way from America to pick cherries in deserted orchards or yawn over a newspaper in a Ford which never moved an inch from one day to the other. They did not realize that one of the severest trials in war is boredom, that action is comparatively rare and that boredom predominates. What they wanted, what most of them had signed up for, was excitement, instead of which they were told to sit down and be patient. By the end of the first week, some harsh things were being said about Triaucourt.

At last our chief, Mr. Ware, got his orders from Paris and we were told to get ready to leave for an undisclosed destination, but we knew we were going east, and going east meant excitement. So we cranked our cars and fifteen minutes later there was not one American left in Triaucourt.

It was not very long before we began hearing the distant sound of cannonade above the rumble of our cars, and villages in ruins told us clearly that we were entering the war zone. One small town through which we drove had been so completely and thoroughly destroyed that nothing remained to indicate that human beings had once lived there, except heaps of stones and a sign giving the name of the locality. That is, I believe, what the Germans call *Vernichtung*.

Towards the end of the afternoon, we reached Clermont-en-Argonne, where we were to take up our quarters for an indefinite length of time. Needless to say, the town had been abandoned in the early stages of the war and the military authorities gave us the largest and finest house in the place. It belonged to a notary, as I soon found out from some books which the unfortunate man had not been able to take away. We slept in the rooms on the second floor, ate ravenously of the excellent food which was served to us, and grew more and more impatient as the days went by and none of us were sent to the front.

There were two French soldiers and a French lieutenant attached to our section. Of course, the men did not understand English, but the lieutenant did. One day when we were particularly rowdy because it had been raining since dawn and we had stayed in (and we were beginning to hate Clermont as much as we hated Triaucourt), one of the soldiers asked his officer what was the matter with us. "They are annoyed because they haven't been sent to the front yet," the lieutenant answered. The men said nothing, but they looked at each other in a way I shall never forget. Both of them had fought at Verdun.

On the following day, excitement was provided for us in a mild form: we were told that some enemy planes were

166

above Clermont and might bomb our house since our cars were clearly visible all around it. Now I come to think of it, it might have been just as well to leave the house for a while, but for some reason we didn't. Everyone stayed in the dining room except me. I went upstairs and sat on my cot, preferring to be alone. One of our men, I am sorry to say, was so overcome by fright that he had a fit and had to be taken down to the cellar. The next day he was sent back to Paris, in disgrace. It was I who took him to the station, and I shook hands with him as warmly as I could, because I thought he had been unfairly reproved for something which he could not help.

War experiences are as a rule so dull that I cannot bring myself to dwell on mine at great length, although I feel that they have enriched me in many ways. I shall therefore be as brief as I can.

Summer drew to a close and still we had not seen any action. After dark, when everything was quiet, I used to go to the foot of the garden and stand on a terrace overlooking a valley. Then, through the stillness of the night, a low, rumbling sound reached my ears, the distant thunder of Verdun. It never seemed to stop or diminish in intensity; one could hear it every night; it was impossible to imagine that it could go on forever and yet I could not see why it should ever relent. I listened to it with a beating heart and watched the sinister glimmering just above the horizon. This spoke far more than anything I had ever read or heard about the war, and I felt that the years to come could never obliterate this moment from my memory.

By October, they began sending us to certain points of the Argonne forest where it was thought that our help might be needed, although that sector was quiet enough for the moment. On alternate nights, two ambulances were dispatched, each one carrying two men. I was very eager to go and finally my turn came; but Mr. Ware being still a little suspicious of my driving, I was not allowed to do more than sit by the driver. The latter, whom I shall call Johnson, was a theological student, a Unitarian, and spoke very little except when the subject of religion was mentioned, whereupon his bony face would glow and his steel rimmed spectacles glitter as if, in some unaccountable way, they shared his metaphysical raptures. He and I rarely exchanged views, but we were friendly.

We left Clermont and, having driven for a mile or two, reached the road which led to the forest of Argonne. It was a pitch black night and we were, of course, not allowed to use any other kind of light than a torch. Now our difficulties began. The road had been badly shelled and was riddled with holes, some of them large enough to contain a man. Indeed we soon found out that the enemy had not yet lost interest in this road, for a shell whined occasionally above our heads and exploded in the fields on our right. In spite of this we could not move very fast, although our instinct prompted us both to open the throttle as wide as we could in order to reach a safer spot. "You had better get out and direct me," said Johnson. "When you come to a hole, whistle and I'll stop." I obeyed. Whenever I came to a shell-hole, I blew my whistle with all my might and felt tremendously important. Not once did it enter my mind that we could be hit by a shell. So on we crept for half an hour or so, circumventing shell-holes until we reached the forest where, for some reason, we felt quite safe, as if the trees were protecting us.

That night, we slept in a dug-out. Our beds were hardly raised above the ground; very primitive beds they were, made of a few boards hastily nailed together and a straw mattress. There was a table and a chair in one corner, an army blanket over the door to keep out the draughts, and on the ground, between two beds, a lantern which we were advised not to blow out; I soon understood why.

It was early and we talked a little before turning in. Once in a while, we heard the strange hollow whistle of shells above the trees, but apart from that, the air was absolutely still. It seemed extraordinary to me to be in a dug-out with Johnson, and I am sure he felt the same way. I don't think he liked the place very much; all of a sudden he began talking about his home. He took off his glasses

169

and wiped them. It was strange, his talking this way. Then he said something about religion and I grew more interested. He spoke of the enormous power which lies hidden in the Gospel and how the world would be affected by it in future times. The next thing he said took my breath away: he did not believe that there ever had been such a person as Christ, and it did not matter one way or the other, so long as we had the Gospels. What I answered, I do not remember, but I do know that I went to bed feeling extremely puzzled.

We did not undress, so as to be ready to leave immediately if a call came for us. Hardly had we lain down and ceased to talk when the reason for keeping the lantern burning made itself clear. Two or three very large rats began running about in the dark corners of the dug-out. Although at first they kept clear of the light, they soon became accustomed to it and all but upset it in their scurrying. I watched them for a minute and fell asleep.

I do not think more than an hour could have elapsed when a French soldier came and woke us up, saying that there had been a call from a hospital in the neighborhood to transfer a wounded man to a more important sanitary base. So we jumped out of bed and left the dug-out, rubbing our eyes as we went. Quite a few shells whistled over our heads, and each time we fell flat on our stomachs as we had been told to do. Presently we came to the clearing where we had left our car, but the car wasn't there.

Thinking we had made a mistake in the location, we began walking through the woods, occasionally turning on the small flashlights which we were allowed to use, and it was not very long before I spied a strange object at my feet: it was a large fragment of wood painted gray, with a number which I instantly recognized as that of my ambulance. Now we looked in earnest and soon found scattered fragments of the lost Ford which a shell had apparently struck square in the middle and sent flying all over the woods. A great number of fragments were found later in the trees. There was nothing to do but to take the other car (two being sent out daily, as I have explained) and drive to the hospital, which we did.

By the end of the month, all of us having had a taste of war, we were sent to places a little nearer the front lines. The most uncomfortable of these places was a little village called Neuvilly. To be precise, nothing remained of this village except its name which was written on a sign-post near the spot where the Mairie had stood. Several times a day, in a perfunctory sort of way, this desolate spot was shelled, it being known to the Germans that first aid to the wounded was given there in a shelter. Early in October, my turn came to go to Neuvilly. I had been given numerous instructions by Mr. Ware, and during the time of respite drove to the shelter with a thrill of excitement.

I was greeted by a French officer whose name was, let us say, Jalin. Lieutenant Jalin was one of the strangest characters I have ever met. He was about thirty and seemed overjoyed at finding out that I spoke French as well as he did, because, he said, my American comrades were incomprehensible and he was dying of boredom from lack of conversation.

"I am very sorry I can't put you up comfortably," he said as we stepped down into a cellar. "You will have to sleep on one of your own stretchers, over there," (he pointed to a dark corner) "but," he added with a gracious smile, "I can provide you with a pair of sheets. There is nothing like sleeping between sheets."

I agreed.

Having showed me my bedroom, he took me to what he called his dining room, which was also in a cellar, but a well-lighted cellar, with a round table, several chairs and a number of books neatly placed on top of a trunk.

"There is a little barn at the back of our place," he said after a few minutes' conversation. "Park your car there, but drive in carefully."

I obeyed. What he called a barn was really little else than a shed, and I instantly understood why I had been told to drive in carefully, when I saw a dead soldier lying on a stretcher. He had been covered up with a blanket.

Memories of Happy Days

I parked my car and went back to the shelter where my host offered me a cup of coffee. It happened that he was a Parisian as I was, and that he lived in the avenue Victor Hugo, not very far from our street. Moreover, we had several friends in common and not an hour had elapsed before we had the impression that we had known each other a long time.

Of course, I did not mention what I had seen in the shed, although my mind reverted to it now and then with mixed feelings of horror and sadness. I remember that we talked about books. Lieutenant Jalin was very fond of literature, particularly poetry. He knew a lot of poetry by heart and regaled me with some of Albert Samain's voluptuous, if mediocre, lines; these he recited with a quick, detached tone of voice and an occasional outburst of enthusiasm which sent the blood to my cheeks. He had a hard, white face with very black hair, and wore the ribbon of the médaille militaire (the highest military award in France) on his shabby uniform.

"You had better stay in the shelter," he said, when I spoke of going out. "We are only a mile from the front lines. It is safer here."

On and on we talked of Anatole France and Pierre Louÿs and Claude Farrère until dinner-time, whereupon the lieutenant's orderly appeared to set the table which, to my surprise, he covered with a tablecloth of the finest texture. It

173

had been quite a long time since I had seen a tablecloth and I could not help looking at this one with a certain degree of admiration; this seemed to flatter my host.

"As you perceive, I am well cared for here by the army administration," he said with a smile. "They send me more winding-sheets than we could possibly need and I keep a few for my own private use. Besides," he added under his breath, "what do the poor fellows care about being wrapped up in a sheet when they are dead?"

This sounded sensible enough, in a gruesome sort of way, and I ate my meal as heartily as I could. We talked for a while after dinner and I retired to my cellar and got into bed. The lieutenant's orderly had made up my bed for me, very neatly, I must say, but although I had looked forward to this moment, some two or three hours before, I now felt differently and knew too much about my sheets to relish the thought of lying between them. They were soft and limp, and seemed to cling to my body in a very disagreeable way. In fact, I was far more frightened in my bed, that night, than I had been on the road with the German shells overhead. However, I was not alone in the cellar, and that was a comfort: only a few feet away from my bed slept the lieutenant's orderly, a well-known character among American ambulance drivers who never called him anything else but Doucement, for reasons which I shall explain.

Doucement had kept a little wine-shop before the war, in some distant southern town. As a consequence, I suppose, he had become an incorrigible tippler, which did not prevent him from fighting like a lion at the battle of the Marne and later at Verdun. Indeed, he gave such an excellent report of himself for more than two years that, as a sort of reward, over and above the Croix de Guerre, he was sent from the hell of Douaumont to relatively quiet Neuvilly. His task was to ride with ambulance men and show them the way from the front to the different hospitals. We were all fond of him. He was a little man with a rubicund face, a bristly chin, and a broad and winning smile. His habitual tipsiness was a source of great merriment to all but never seemed to interfere with the carrying out of his duty.

It might have been thought that he enjoyed driving with us, but no, these expeditions were a nightmare to Doucement, who was otherwise so brave. This was due partly to our proverbially reckless driving, of which we were very proud, partly to the fact that, Doucement's brain being obscured by the enormous quantity of wine he absorbed every day, he never went out with us but he saw imaginary dangers at every hand. He was terrified at the thought that we might overturn or drive into a ditch. Of course, we made the most of this situation and bounced him up and down at a shameless speed on shell-riddled roads. The poor man could do nothing but moan and wail:

"Doucement!" when he considered that his last hour had come.

The fear that he would be killed in a Ford driven by one of those fiendish Americans soon became a sort of obsession with him and even disturbed him in his sleep. Even if I had not been told about this, I would have found it out for myself that night. Not more than a few minutes had elapsed before my companion, who was in his usual happy state of mind when he turned in, began muttering to himself as he tossed on his stretcher. This went on for some time, then the well-known cry rent the air:

"Doucement!"

It was impossible to sleep when Doucement had his familiar nightmare. All one could do was to wait until it came to a climax and the sufferer finally subsided. Waking him up was no help. He had to go through the whole process of being dumped into a ditch, and shaking him by the shoulder was simply postponing the agony by a few minutes. So I lay awake until, after much sighing and sobbing and a long succession of heart-rending *"Doucements,"* the ex-wine merchant had met his death for the hundredth time in a Ford car. This done, he reposed more quietly and I gratefully closed my eyes.

Not for very long. Doucement's nightmare was bad enough, but a more elaborate one was soon to begin. In his

176

conversation with me, before dinner, Lieutenant Jalin had incidentally remarked on the size of rats in this region of France.

"I believe," he said, not without a certain amount of pride, "I believe we have the largest rats in Europe."

I soon discovered that he had not been boasting. There happened to be enough moonlight in our cellar to enable me to observe the size and shape of the huge rodents which I saw silhouetted against the walls as they came out of their holes. Doucement's wailing had kept them away for a while, but now that he had quieted down, they grew bolder and began running between our beds, looking for morsels of food. Some of these animals seemed to me as large as small dogs, and I could think of nothing else to do but draw my blanket (together with my winding-sheet) well over my head. This was not such a good idea, as the rats, seeing that they were undisturbed in their search for food, came closer to my bed and even ran over my body. I finally went to sleep because I was very tired and when one is tired at seventeen not even rats in an Argonne cellar can keep one awake.

So much for my war experiences in France. Towards the end of that month, the Field Service was taken over by the American army and I, being too young by one year, was discharged. I then joined the American Red Cross, still a private organization, which disregarded the fact that I was not eighteen and sent me to the Italian front together with forty other Americans, most of them college men.

Our headquarters were at a medieval village called Roncade, not very far from Treviso and almost equally near Venice. We were comfortably lodged in villas and did little else but stand and wait, hoping that we also served. The battle of the Isonzo was over, the Italian retreat had been stopped by the French, and there was little probability that the German High Command would order another push in that section of Europe, so everything pointed to an uneventful winter, and I bought as many books as I could in the neighboring town in order to pass the time as pleasantly as possible.

Once and once only we were allowed to go to Venice. To see Venice for the first time at the age of seventeen — well, whatever dreams I had, and I lived much in my dreams, this surpassed them all. Here was nothing but beauty of such rare and exquisite quality that I could only gape and wonder at every step. I don't know how Venice struck my companions, but to me it was like awaking to a new life. Wherever the war might be in Europe, it was not here, in spite of the sand bags that reminded one of the possibility of an air raid. A gondola took me up and down the narrow canals where even the rags hanging in the sunlight seemed lovely, and I felt so happy that no words could adequately have expressed what went on in me. It was as if

178

every impression of sadness which had been made on my mind since I was born was miraculously wiped out like something that is effaced from a blackboard. The reason I dwell on this is that nothing in later life ever gave me a pleasure of that particular quality and I cannot help acknowledging my debt to Italy for one of the greatest moments I have ever experienced. I understood the wonder that filled the half-civilized French soldiers of Louis XII's army when they poured into the plains of Lombardy and I really felt that in some indescribable way I had all of a sudden been born again.

My room at Roncade was paved with marble, but fortunately the winter was mild and I was able to work most of the time by an open window. I wrote stories and poems which, I am glad to say, I had the sense to destroy. Twice a week, I was sent out in my ambulance to report at various hospitals but not once were my services required, for the simple reason that there were no casualties. I was thankful, nevertheless, for the opportunity to see such cities as Treviso and Padua.

In the early part of February, I received a letter from my father telling me that my sister Retta had died. She was twenty-two and overwork at the hospital had proved fatal. Both she and Anne had been awarded medals for distinguished service, the seldom given Médaille des Epidémies.

CHAPTER SIX

Having signed up for six months, I was discharged in May and went back to Paris after a few weeks' stay in Rome, where I visited my sister Mary. It felt strange to be home again. To be sure, our home had not changed, but I had, and I wondered what turn my life was going to take. In spite of American aid, the end of the war seemed far out of sight and the strength of the German military machine still tremendous, as had been proved in the preceding March offensive when the Franco-British front had almost been cleaved asunder. There was no reason to believe that the war could not go on almost indefinitely, now that everyone had accepted it and that our daily life had become adjusted to this monstrous state of things. It appeared likely, therefore, that sooner or later, for better or for worse, I would enter the army.

I allowed myself a month's holiday to make up my mind. My father did not try to influence me in one way or the other. He talked about the war in a calmly optimistic manner which gave us all much confidence. No words can express his contempt for the Germans — not that he had ever doubted their courage on the battle-field, "but," he said, "when things begin to go wrong, the German morale deteriorates. Success is indispensable to the Germans if they are to keep up the struggle. Unlike the British, they waver and lose confidence in the face of defeat. But if all goes well, they are first-rate soldiers."

Although he hated their thirst for conquest, he admired their spirit of discipline and self-sacrifice, and also the accuracy with which they carried out orders. At that time, Paris was being shelled every day by Big Bertha, the long range gun, and no one in France has forgotten what dreadful havoc this deadly weapon worked on the church of Saint-Gervais, on the afternoon of Good Friday, 1918. The roof of the church was shattered and a great many people were killed or injured. However, apart from this shocking crime which our enemies considered a very happy hit, comparatively few casualties were reported and everyone seemed to become accustomed to the daily visitation. Ordinarily, the shelling took place at five P.M. sharp. A shell burst at the foot of our street and did little damage. I happened to be at home at the time. My father was in the drawing room with his watch in his hand, and when the shell exploded, on the stroke of five, he merely said, not without a certain note of admiration:

"I declare, those fellows are remarkable. Always on the dot!"

A great many American boys came to see us during that year, friends or relatives, all in uniform. My cousin Sarah, who was a nurse at the American hospital of Neuilly, gave parties several times a week, in spite of, or, I might say, because of circumstances. It will seem strange to some that while so many men were risking their lives at the front, there should have been so much merry-making in Paris, but it was felt by all that gloom could in no way help the morale of soldiers on leave. So dances were held and every effort was made to forget the horror of the times.

One day, a friend of mine who was an ex-ambulance man came to see us in a beautifully cut French uniform. He explained that, although American, he had been allowed to join the French artillery and was studying at the artillery school of Fontainebleau, which he expected to leave with a gold stripe on his sleeve. There were over forty Americans at the school and it took very little talking on my friend's part to persuade me to join them. Some time after that conversation, I appeared in front of a board of French officers and told them I wanted to enlist.

As a foreigner, I could not be allowed to join the French army, but this difficulty was neatly got around by first having me sign up in the Foreign Legion (in which I remained for the space of an hour), and then transferring me from the Legion into the regular army. In due time I was equipped with a "horizon blue" uniform, top boots and spurs which impressed me beyond words.

At Fontainebleau, where I was sent shortly after, I met several boys from the Field Service and the Red Cross. Their reason for joining the French instead of the American army was, I think, that they would be promoted to the rank of *aspirant* (equivalent to that of second lieutenant) at the end of six months' study, provided, of course, they passed the examinations, whereas obtaining a commission in the American army would have implied (unless I am mistaken) going back to the States and entering one of the military schools in that country. They were anxious to see some action (there were strong indications by this time that the German resistance was slowly giving in) and wanted to be sent to the front as soon as possible.

Our barracks were as clean and comfortable as could be expected and the food wholesome and plentiful, the French army, as usual, being given the best of everything in wartime. In the morning we were taken to the drill field where we were taught what there is to know about the 75 and 155 millimeter guns, how to point them and, at a later stage of the course, how to fire them. Cotton was provided for our ears. In the afternoon, we attended lectures on ballistics and learned how to solve problems of "adjustment" as rapidly as possible. All of which seemed extremely difficult to me who am anything but mathematically minded. I may as well say right now that I was a very poor student at the Artillery School and that, in all probability, I would never had been allowed to go to the front as an officer when I left Fontainebleau, had there still been a front at that time.

Our task was made as easy as it could be by the almost incredible patience and good nature of our teacher. His name was Roland. A more typical Frenchman than Lieutenant Roland could not have been found between Boulogne and Marseille. His gaiety, his wit, his kind brown eyes, his delightful Midi accent and the slightly ribald jokes with which he interspersed his speech, everything about him endeared him to us. He also had that eminently French gift of making the most complicated matters as clear as crystal and of imparting knowledge without being dull. Nevertheless, I retained little of what he taught us. I think he liked his students — it is very seldom that a Frenchman does not get along with Americans — and we certainly thought of him as a friend. He never said anything disagreeable; he evidently believed that roaring at men only confuses them and that teaching with a smile is more effective. I can only wish that this intelligent Frenchman's method were more widespread.

From five o'clock on we were free to do what we wanted
184

and I usually profited by this to go and sit in the lovely gardens of the Château. I always had a copy of Baudelaire in my pocket and read my favorite poet (he still is) whose lines had become so familiar to me that they were almost a part of my mental make-up. A more exquisite use of French words did not seem possible, nor have years altered my opinion on that subject. The romantic glory of the sunsets together with the classical design of these seventeenth century gardens seemed reflected in some way in the melancholy poems whose sober perfection filled me then, as now, with ever increasing wonder. Here was something which urged me to express myself and I longed to be able to write, but it was useless even to think of such things while I had the intricacies of ballistics to cope with.

Events, however, were moving rapidly and at the end of a few weeks we were all persuaded that we would never be sent to the front. Nevertheless, the 11th of November came as an almost incredible surprise. Germany had at last been brought to her knees, but I don't think anyone among us suspected that, by asking for an armistice, our dangerous enemy had succeeded in saving his skin. Our joy was tempered by a great disappointment: we were not allowed to go up to Paris and witness one of the greatest moments in the history of the world; we had to be content with the celebrations at Fontainebleau. The crowd assembled in front of the Mairie, the façade of which was illuminated with small lanterns of different colors. There was no shouting, no wild waving of flags; men and women smiled with the slightly dazed expression of people who have awaked from a dream and have not yet succeeded in readjusting their thoughts to the world of reality.

The next day, we crowded around our lieutenant like school-children.

"Do we have to go on?" we asked.

He looked at us round-eyed.

"Of course," he said, "of course, *mes amis*. Your help may yet be needed."

So we piled into our truck and drove to the field, but the 75 mm gun seemed like a toy which we had out-grown.

A few weeks later, we passed our final tests, but I suspect that our examiners had received instructions to be particularly lenient and to pass us all. Be that as it may, we were now allowed to wear a bit of gold braid on our sleeve and privates had to salute us; but we felt cheated. We were sent to Paris where we were told to await our marching orders unless we chose to be demobilized immediately. My father urged me to join my regiment, although I felt little inclined to do so. By this time, I had had enough of army life and was aching to get back into civilian clothes for good. Paris seemed even more attractive than it had ever been in my eyes and I hated to leave it again. "But," said my father, "you are being given a splendid opportunity to travel and see new countries. Your regiment is to be sent to the Rhineland. This is an experience which you should not miss."

So I packed my small black trunk once more and the next morning drove to the Gare de l'Est where I obtained a ticket to Metz. In that city, my regiment had established its headquarters. Metz in the snow and the mud was a bleak enough place, but fortunately I did not have to stay there as I found that my regiment had moved on to the north of Strasbourg. Another train took me to Haguenau, but it appeared that my regiment was always quicker than had been anticipated, for when I reached Haguenau, all that remained of the unit to which I belonged was a captain who sat in a stuffy little office scribbling behind fortifications of letters and reports. When he heard that I was American, he looked up and said: "*Ah, vous êtes Américain?*" very much like the Parisian in *Les Lettres Persanes* who, seeing a Persian for the first time, is reported to have said: "*Ah, Monsieur est Persan? Comment fait-on pour être Persan?*" I half expected my captain to ask me: "*Comment fait-on pour être Américain?*" but he didn't, he simply examined me behind his pince-nez and gave me my marching orders with an amiable smile.

My regiment was quartered in a village almost on the German border. No train could carry me there, but towards

187

the end of that afternoon, an old-fashioned buggy picked me up at the corner of a street and we trotted away into the country. For some reason, that drive has remained in my memory more vividly than other incidents of greater importance, probably because of the exceptional beauty of the landscape around us. The driver was a Breton, like most of the men in my regiment. He was anything but garrulous and I was not inclined to conversation, so we drove in complete silence for several hours. It had been snowing steadily the preceding day and the white fields gleamed softly in the twilight. There was, I remember, something almost magical in the quality of the air, in the stillness of everything. From under the top of the carriage, I could see the stars shining in the sky which had now become black, and we moved on and on through the dazzling whiteness of the snow. My fingers were numb with cold, but an unaccountable feeling of happiness had crept over me and I did not care whether we drove on right through the night. Why I felt so happy, I would have been at great pains to explain. We passed very few houses and, owing probably to the fact that there was little or nothing to diversify what we could see from the road, I soon lost all sense of time; I dozed a little, lulled to sleep by the rumble of the wheels, and woke up to find that we were apparently at the same point as when I lost consciousness, with the snow casting its mysterious glimmer towards the sky, and

188

the stars looking down on us in what I fancied was a friendly way.

It was almost midnight when we drove into the narrow square of an Alsatian village. The gabled houses were watching the stone fountain as they had done for three centuries; nothing seemed to have changed here since the days of Louis XIV when the province had been annexed to the crown of France. It was like stepping out of our times into a conventional, old-fashioned painting of an ideal village, and I could only gaze in childish delight at what I saw. There was a lantern hanging in the middle of the square and gently swaying in the wind, a wrought-iron sign in the shape of a crown over the inn, and, on top of the fountain, a stone soldier holding a halberd. The snow, in some way, made everything complete.

Our carriage had stopped in front of a small house by the Mairie. I walked in and was given a hearty welcome by three French officers who had waited up all evening for me. As I had never seen them in my life, I wondered at their cordiality, which was explained, however, a little later. There was a lieutenant, a second lieutenant and an aspirant like myself. I have forgotten the second lieutenant's name, but the lieutenant, a black-eyed Breton, was called Bienassis. The aspirant's name was Bro de Comères; he was a handsome boy whose parents lived in Paris, in the avenue de l'Alma. Having been offered a chair by the fire

189

and a glass of *eau de vie*, I was politely asked a few questions about myself, and, as I answered, I saw my companions smile and nod at each other. Finally, the lieutenant exclaimed: "You don't realize what a relief it is to hear you speak! We had been told a week ago that we would be sent an American, and ever since we have been trying to imagine what you were like. We certainly didn't expect you to speak French intelligibly!"

So we talked and laughed for a while and went to bed. We were comfortably lodged and I soon became quite attached to our village, but three days later our marching orders came and we had to leave. This caused much annoyance to my fellow aspirant, who was honoring with his attentions the Lutheran minister's daughter, but we consoled him by saying that Germany was full of Lutheran ministers with plenty of daughters who would no doubt be glad to teach him German.

That afternoon we crossed the border. All four of us rode abreast with the guns rumbling behind us. How strange it felt to be riding on horseback into Germany! My companions seemed to take it as a matter of course. To be invaded and to invade, they had that in their blood, but not I. I found it difficult to realize that all this was true. As we went through the German villages, we were watched by women on the door-steps and dozens of fair-haired children about them. There were very few men to be seen

and no signs of hostility anywhere. It must not be forgotten, however, that the Saar region through which we were
passing was anything but unfriendly to the French, as I
shall have occasion to remark later. Hatred, if hatred there
was, could be found only further back in Germany.

Never did I hear my companions speak in anger of our
conquered foe. It was during our march through the Saar
that Lieutenant Bienassis told me how he had been made
prisoner in 1915 and had escaped from Germany early in
1918. Others had suffered from ill treatment at the hands
of the Germans, but not he, and I remember his telling us
that, at the time of the Kronprinz's ineffectual efforts to
storm Verdun, a German officer came up to his French
prisoner with a paper in his hand, saying with a hard Prus-
sian accent: "*Monsieur, vous vous battez bien!*" This story
and others of the kind made a deep impression on me and
convinced me of the fact that soldiers of nations at war are
not infrequently capable of a certain regard for each other,
as if there were a sort of international *esprit de corps* tran-
scending at times the borders of hostile countries. But this,
alas, is not generally true, as the French prisoners of 1940
can testify.

We were three days reaching our destination, there being apparently no reason why we should hurry. The country we traveled through was one of meadows, brooks and
rolling hills, altogether pleasant. Occasionally we came to

an industrial town where miners with blackened faces would silently watch us as we rode up the streets. I was curious to know what they thought, but of course there was no way of finding out. Did they resent our presence? Did they hate us? If they did, they never showed it. Only the women looked a little alarmed and held their children close to them, but apparently their curiosity was greater than their fear, for they crowded the streets.

At last we arrived at a village called Nieder Linxweiler, only a few miles from Neunkirchen. The guns were placed in a field beyond the village and we were billeted with orders to cause as little annoyance as possible to the inhabitants. The room to which I was assigned was in a house at the end of Main Street. I cannot say that I got along well with the owners of the house, because I never saw them or even caught a glimpse of them. Sometimes I heard them talk in a low voice in the room next to mine; apart from this, they never made their presence known. By a sort of tacit understanding, I seldom was in my room during the day. My breakfast was brought to me by my orderly, a foolish but likeable boy from Angers, called Jarras. He made up my bed and swept the floor; I may add that my room was simply but comfortably furnished, with an iron bed, a basin and pitcher, and a few pious pictures on the walls.

Most of my time was spent in the house where we took

our meals. It was a picturesque old farm with a beautiful water-mill which was used in normal times for grinding seed. The dining room, which we turned into our living room, had a window looking out on fields and woods and was pleasant enough, though small. It had a round table with a pink oil cloth on it, straw-bottomed chairs, a china stove, and on the wall a large engraving of Leonardo's Last Supper under which was written: *Amen, dico vobis quia unus ex vobis traditurus est me.* All these details come back to me so vividly after twenty-two years that I could almost fancy I had left the place a month ago. As we were all pretty talkative and had many stories to tell, our meals were always very gay and by the end of the first week, I felt as if I had known my companions since childhood.

There was little to do in the afternoon but walk or ride, and I soon came to know the neighborhood fairly well, in spite of a strangely defective sense of direction which I have never been able to improve and which, more than once, took me out of my way. My one acquaintance among the population was a plump and fiercely respectable girl who taught school at a nearby village. How I met her, I can't remember, but I do know that once a week I went to her house in the afternoon and was treated to a cup of ersatz-coffee and waffles which she made in my honor. Her father, I may add, was perpetually lurking in the hall or in one of the back rooms. I never saw him, but Fräulein

193

Effi assured me that he was very friendly to the invaders, as indeed, she said, were most of the inhabitants of the village. *"Aber,"* she added, "we are not *echte Deutsche*. The real Germans are in Berlin."

We discussed poetry. She liked Schiller and I liked Goethe. I wish now that I had spent less time arguing about authors I knew so little, instead of asking my hostess to tell me how she and her neighbors had fared during the war; thus might I have learned something of interest, but I suppose I wanted to make an impression.

One day, I arrived at Fräulein Effi's and found that she had another guest, a middle-aged lady who, it appeared, lived at Trier. There was an awkward moment as I instantly realized that the lady was anything but well disposed towards the army of occupation. The steel-like quality of the look she gave me told me more about the way she felt than the longest speech could have done. At last Fräulein Effi introduced me, whereupon the lady rose and coming up to me spoke as follows:

"Young man, although you are an enemy to my country, I cannot say that I hate the French nation. England is the only country I hate, not France. Your hand!"

I gave her my hand which she shook with furious energy. Tears stood in her blue eyes and I could not help but feel sorry for her, but said nothing. Without adding a word, she nodded to Fräulein Effi and departed.

Memories of Happy Days

"My friend has a good heart, but she is *taktlos, nicht?*"
said Fräulein Effi as she came back from the front door.

I expressed no opinion on the subject and did not stay
very long that day. The events of 1939 shed a curious
light on this little incident.

Early in the spring of 1919, I was demobilized and went home. What my life was to be and how I was going to earn my living did not bother me very much, owing to a deep-rooted conviction that everything would be all right and that fate had decided to deal kindly with me. Of course, I should have to choose some kind of profession. My father had gently hinted that, sooner or later, a decision had to be reached in this matter, but I found it difficult to make up my mind. I really wanted to be a painter or, as second best choice, a writer; in no case would I consider going into business.

Well then, I would paint. That meant that I must not only buy an easel, canvases, paint-brushes and tubes of paint, but also find a good place to paint in, an atelier — painting in my dark bedroom being out of the question — and the expense would be staggering to a young man with only fifty francs as a monthly allowance. Also it was not inconceivable, in spite of my enormous self-confidence,

196

that I might have to take a few lessons, if only to learn how to mix my colors. More money would be required and the war had anything but enriched us. Never mind, thought I, the A B C of painting is to look at pictures. With this highly questionable theory in mind, I decided to go to the Louvre every day, which I did faithfully for five months, examining only ten or twelve pictures of a morning, but with much care. Thus did I ease my conscience; whenever it asked me, as it sometimes did: "What are you doing with your time? How are you building up your future?" I answered triumphantly: "Why, I am studying art!" And being a good-natured conscience, it was appeased by these words for a time.

My visual memory was good and I loved color. By the end of July, I had become familiar with most of the pictures on the second floor of the Louvre, even with the seldom looked at baroque paintings in the long gallery that runs along the Seine. After lengthy meditations, I had decide that El Greco was to be my model, although that painter was represented by only two pictures in the whole museum. Of course, I knew perfectly what my own pictures were going to be like, but this was a secret which I never imparted to anyone. I wanted the whole thing to be a surprise. "People will see," I said to myself. I flattered myself that there were no limits to my ambition, and as I looked admiringly at King Ferdinando's bare arm coming

197

out of his cuirass and holding a scepter, I felt convinced that I could do almost as well, and that people would see; but I prudently refrained from trying.

I do not regret the hours devoted to these delusions of grandeur: they enabled me to acquire a certain knowledge of the history of painting and developed in me whatever taste I had for art, but I have yet to know what it feels like to hold a paint-brush and a palette.

Towards the middle of August, my father received a letter from my Uncle Walter Hartridge, who was solicitor general at Savannah, and judging from the expression on my father's face, it bore excellent news. By way of thanking him for taking care of his niece Sarah Elliott who had come over to spend two months with us and had spent twelve years, Uncle Walter offered to send me to an American university, which offer was gratefully and immediately accepted.

I received this piece of news in silence. To leave France, and above all to leave Paris, was, I considered, the end of everything as far as I was concerned; but it seemed to matter very little what my feelings on the subject might be, and the next day a passage was secured for me on the *Rochambeau,* sailing September 10th from Marseille.

What went on in my mind was indescribable. Although my ship did not leave for a month, I ran to bid a dramatic good-bye to my friends, particularly to my old classmate

Gilbert who wrote in *vers libres* about the Paris churches, in spite of the fact that he was an atheist and something of a bolshevik. He was a serious young man with strong feelings about people's wrongs and firm hopes as to the coming world revolution. When I told him that I might have to spend three years in America, he frowned ominously:

"You must say no!" he exclaimed. "You must revolt!"

I pointed out that revolting would mean being put into business, and wasn't that even more horrible? This question was thrashed out tumultuously and it was finally agreed that to revolt, although it had much about it that was attractive, might not be the wisest course, in the present case. So after several long tirades, Gilbert finally abandoned me to my fate, and we parted, not without having exchanged vows of undying friendship.

The *Rochambeau* had been booked entirely by the American Red Cross. Four or five hundred nurses, doctors and ambulance drivers, all eager to go home, trouped into the ship on the morning of September 19th, and I among them. My cousin Sarah, also a member of the American Red Cross, had availed herself of this opportunity to return to the States, and was all excitement, as indeed was everyone else. I tried, with little success, to share in the general exuberance. I was still very self-conscious when I spoke English, and my accent betrayed me; also it bored me to have to explain that I was American and then to be told that I looked like a Frenchman. Nevertheless, I soon found out that most of the people on board were likeable for some reason or other.

Our trip was a very roundabout one. We sailed from Marseille in a blaze of sunlight and I looked with a heavy heart at the shores of France as they faded away in the glory of noon. Our first stop was Naples and we were allowed a whole day ashore while the ship refueled. Instead of sailing away in a noisy motorboat like everyone else, I was taken to the wharf in a small rowboat. Why, I can't remember, but it was so. Perhaps I preferred to do my sightseeing alone. Be that as it may, I shall never forget that the boat I was in was manned by an old sailor and a young boy, the latter suggesting (after having exchanged winks with the old sailor) that if I cared to meet his *sorella*, a meeting could immediately and conveniently be arranged for the modest sum of twenty *lire*; he then proceeded to explain why it might be desirable for me to know his sister and I, having some Italian, turned crimson and refused. Whereupon remarks (unkind remarks, I fear) were made about me in Neapolitan dialect. As soon as we reached the wharf, I hurried away as quickly as I could, and with a map of the city in my hands found my way to the via Toledo and the Museum.

We pulled out of Naples that night and made for Palermo which we reached on the following day. A few hours only were allowed us ashore, and in that short space of time I tried to crowd in as many baroque palaces and Byzantine churches as I could: After this we sailed due west and did not stop before we arrived at New York.

As this book is not a book of travel, I shall not dwell very long on my first impression of New York, which, I suppose, did not differ very much from most people's. The skyline of that city filled me with amazement. There was something so strange and unearthly about these rows of stone giants in the morning light that I could only look at them with a mixture of admiration and alarm, and found no words to express what I felt. What I saw did not look like a human city — it was out of all proportion to any city I had ever seen before — but it had beauty, a monstrous, terrible sort of beauty; it was like a Venice built by Martians, or the capital of a nation of cyclops. What could be the mentality of a people who built themselves such tremendous houses to live in? I felt all of a sudden like a medieval man confronted for the first time with the modern world. "How," I asked myself, "how will I ever manage to feel at home among skyscrapers?"

We finally landed and my cousin told me to go and look for my uncle while she attended to her luggage. I therefore walked the length of the pier and sure enough there was my uncle waiting for us in the crowd. He was standing against a railing, a tall, handsome man, blinking a little as he always did. I knew him immediately, having seen him eight years before when he came to France and paid us a visit, but he did not know me, which was natural as I had changed considerably since the age of eleven. What followed will seem, I feel sure, incredible to many. I walked up to my uncle and, just as I was about to speak to him, was seized with an unconquerable fit of shyness and turned away.

"Well?" asked Sarah when I came back. "Well, you had better come along," I said with a blush. "I'd hate to go up to the wrong person and say, 'Hello, Uncle.'" She waved her hand and tried to expostulate, but I was very firm. The truth is that I was terrified of my Uncle Walter. All my life I had been told what a remarkable person he was, what a brilliant orator, what an energetic and important man, and although inferiority complexes had not yet been invented, I had one just the same and mine, if I may say so, was a beauty.

There was no reason to be frightened of my uncle, however. He was as kind and unpretentious a man as I have ever met and did everything in his power to make me feel happy in America, as I shall try to show later on. He had come up from Savannah with my aunt and when I finally nerved myself into shaking hands with him, appeared so pleased to see me that I felt ashamed of not having spoken to him right away. My aunt was there too, and her *gentillesse* (if I may be allowed to lapse into French) did much to make me feel at ease. She had little trouble in guessing how bewildered I was, and perceiving that I was practically tongue-tied from self-consciousness, she tactfully did most of the talking. May she be rewarded for it!

A few hours later, I was walking up Fifth Avenue in a dazed condition and only half believing what my eyes saw as they looked up at the skyscrapers. That evening, I went to the theater with Sarah. We saw *The Jest* with John and Lionel Barrymore. Never having heard English spoken on the stage, I missed almost all of the first act, when suddenly I was able to understand every word. This was a strange experience which reminded me of the day when, having pondered for months over the alphabet, I realized that I could read. The play was an Italian melo-drama in a renaissance setting with as many daggers, poi-soned cups of wine and serenades as could reasonably be expected, and I came away fully convinced that the Barry-mores were the greatest actors alive.

The next day, my aunt went back to Savannah with Sarah, and towards the end of that afternoon, my uncle and I took the train to Washington, our destination being the University of Virginia. At Washington, we boarded what I later found out was called the Virginia Creeper and in the dead of night we reached Charlottesville. It was raining; my uncle felt tired and said little; we drove in

silence from the station to the Monticello Hotel, where
we spent the rest of the night. As I woke up the next morning, I looked out of my window and saw the old court
house with its white pillars and pediment and a Civil War
gun dreaming of Manassas in the September sun. This was
my first glimpse of the South and for some reason it moved
me more than anything else of the kind ever did. Words
spoken by my mother came back to me after many years;
it was as if the world she had loved stood before me in a
kind of simplified picture, and in a curious way I recognized this picture because I was looking at it through her
eyes.

After breakfast, we took the street-car to the University and walked up the long stone path that leads to the
Rotunda. It was a fine clear day and I was struck by the
loveliness of the grounds, but I was too excited to speak,
and as my uncle was anything but talkative, we made our
way in deep silence to the registrar's office. There, with a
pounding heart, I read the card which I was asked to fill
out. How strange everything seemed to me! Only three
weeks before, I was walking in the streets of Paris, and
now . . . One of the questions asked on this card was the
name of the person by whom the student had been entered
at the University as well as the degree of relationship exist-
ing between the two. So I wrote "Walter Hartridge" and
underneath, "Uncle." So flustered was I, however, that I

spelt Uncle with a K. Unkle. I was in a confused state of mind; my face burned and my collar felt like a halter. Had I been asked if I was really and truly Julian Green, I would in all probability have answered "No." The only thing that roused me was that, seeing the name of Paris as the place of my birth, the registrar asked me if that was Paris, Texas Whereupon I replied that I had never heard of Paris, Texas, and that as far as I knew there was but one Paris in the world. Only a terrified person could have been so gratuitously rude, but my incredible awkwardness was constantly creating uncomfortable situations. I was appalled at my own impertinence. Blush upon blush suffused my cheeks. My uncle and the registrar exchanged smiles and it was explained that I was born in France.

No sooner had we left the registrar's office than it occurred to me that "Uncle" might look better spelt with a *c*. I forget what reason I gave my uncle for running back to the office, but run back I did, asked for my card and corrected my mistake, inwardly vowing that if I had anything to do with it, the registrar and I would never again come face to face in this world.

The next thing to do was to find me a room, but of course, the University having opened three weeks before, all the best rooms had been taken and I had to be content with one on Fourteenth Street. My windows commanded a perfect view of the B. & O. bridge which ran so near the house that whenever a train went thundering by I had the impression that my bed lay across the track; more alarming yet, to my unaccustomed European ears, was the loud and impatient clangor of the bell. My uncle regretted that better lodgings were not available, but he gave me far more money than I needed and advised me to move to some other place as soon as I could. With these and other comforting words, he shook hands with me and departed.

At that age, I found it painful to have to meet anyone, and it proved doubly trying in a country where, in many ways, I felt like a foreigner. However, I suppose it did me good, like most unpleasant experiences. I had to make myself go up to people I had never seen and explain who I was. Excessive nervousness played tricks on me, compelling me, for instance, to force myself upon students whom I did not care to know and to avoid sedulously those whom I felt anxious to meet. I wanted friends and seemed to do everything I could in order to be alone. There was something in me which always interfered with my saying exactly what I wanted; rather did I feel inspired to bring about situations which I dreaded. Whenever a step forward was expected and tacitly encouraged, I stood still, or retreated. I was disagreeable to those I wanted to please and ingratiated myself with bores from whom everybody fled. This gaucherie, I imagine, is not uncommon in very young men, but I carried it to a degree which would seem unbelievable if I were to describe it. As a result of this strange state of mind, I was miserably lonely and poured out my unhappiness in long, melancholy letters to my friend Gilbert.

English, German, Latin and Greek were the courses I chose. I eschewed Mathematics, which I loathed, and proceeded to study as hard as I could, partly from a natural love of books, partly because I fancied that in this way I might kill time more effectively than by mooning. Had anyone had the idea of looking for me between the hours of two and six in the afternoon, I might invariably have been found in one of the alcoves of the Rotunda, sitting at one of the heavy oak tables with books on every side. It pleased my vanity to think that I was sitting where, perhaps, Edgar Allan Poe himself had sat before me, and that what I saw, as I looked out of the window, he had also seen and dreamed over, the long row of white pillars bordering the lawn, the terraces and the neo-classic façades of the professors' houses. Here, I thought, was the spot where I was least unhappy. If I could not go back to Paris, as I longed to, I could at least escape from my surroundings by living in a world of my own, serious though this world might be, but I was at an age when one enjoys being serious and taking life in dead earnest. Only the middle-aged succeed in being genuinely frivolous; young men, as a rule, are made of heavier stuff.

When I look back on my first year at the University, I

cannot but feel irritated with myself for my stupidity. I do not mean that I wasted my time; on the contrary, much that I know today, however little that may be, I made my own at the University. Neither can I feel anything but gratitude towards the professors who taught me. But I might have been happy had I only accepted what life offered me with open hands. My thoughts kept reverting to Paris with a kind of morbid obstinacy, blinding me to the fact that I lived in one of the most agreeable spots in the world, without the slightest material care, among people who were kindly disposed toward me and would have had much to give in return for the friendship which I foolishly withheld. It is quite useless now to wish that I might go back to the University and be twenty again with the added experience which I then lacked, but such idle wishes are natural and I confess that I have made them a thousand times.

So my first year was spent in almost complete loneliness. Very few of the men I spoke to were of the kind I might have chosen to confide in: propinquity, not inclination, brought us together. Yet, how I wished for someone to talk to whose tastes and aspirations I could share! I dreamed of an ideal friendship which years could never destroy, but made no real attempts to bring this about.

My holidays were divided between Virginia and

Georgia. At my Uncle Will's house in Prince William
County I passed the warmer part of the summer. It was a
charming old place with fine trees all around it and a view
of the Blue Ridge Mountains. My grandfather had built
the house towards the middle of the last century, on the
edge of what had once been a race course, and called it The
Lawn. Skirmishes had taken place in the vicinity during
the War between the States and bullet holes could still be
seen in the gray weather-board near one of the porches.
The house itself was an oasis of coolness in mid-August
and was filled with souvenirs of bygone days, filled too
with the sound of laughter, for I had numerous cousins
who were anything but melancholy. How much their
gaiety helped me, they probably never suspected, because
I had made a point of honor of never letting anyone know
what went on in my mind, but I longed for their company
even though I spoke but little when I was among them. I
need hardly say how friendly they were to their French
cousin, as they sometimes called me, and I never left The
Lawn without a heavy heart.

My visits to Savannah, where my mother's family came
from, were made briefer by the sub-tropical temperature
to which I was unaccustomed. My uncle lived on one of
those beautiful shady squares which are the pride of the
city and which my mother had so often described to us.
Of course, one of the first visits I paid in Savannah was

to my grandfather's house, sometimes referred to by Northerners as Sherman's headquarters, because Charles Green, who was a British subject, offered his house to the invader in order to spare his Southern friends the humiliation of having their enemy quartered on them. Sherman speaks kindly enough of my grandfather in his memoirs, but they got along wretchedly together. My grandfather's sympathies were decidedly Southern and I may add that he escaped being shot for helping the Southern cause only because he was not an American citizen; he was imprisoned at Fort Warren, Virginia, where he remained several months.

His house, the exterior of which is in Tudor style, is a good specimen of Victorian architecture. I was most struck by the large double drawing-room with its stuccoed ceiling and dark woodwork, but I think that, had the house been mine, I would have spent most of my time in the library, a quiet room with an old-fashioned fireplace and, as I remember, gothic windows looking out into a garden.*

Every morning, I accompanied my uncle to the Court House. I was allowed to sit at a table with the lawyers and watch the trials. Most of the cases were petty larceny and misdemeanors of a minor type, but once in a while we got

* Photographs of this house appeared in an issue of *House and Garden*, in 1939.

a case of rape and not infrequently a murder. I was passionately interested in everything I saw and heard and could never refrain from hoping that the defendant would get off, which, I realize, was unreasonable. Some of the defendants were dreadful criminals against whom society in some way or other had to defend itself, but I inwardly wished them good luck in spite of it all. I could not help imagining what I would have done, had I been in their shoes, facing an imperturbable judge and an angry solicitor whose questions I could not well understand, falling into every legal trap that was set to catch me, contradicting myself because I had forgotten what I had previously said, then being pounced upon and baited until I finally gave up fighting for my life or my freedom. What struck me then was the crudeness of our methods in trying to get at the truth. To be sure, we no longer twist the defendants' hands and feet to obtain a confession, but what we sometimes do morally to defendants is quite on a par with our ancestors' physical brutality. Short of blows, it seems to me that every kind of intimidation is used and I am sure that what we consider dealing fairly with a defendant will make future generations sick, provided future generations are more civilized than we. Having made these remarks, I feel it only just to add that the members of the Savannah bar were as humane as they could possibly be and showed a sincere desire to serve the cause of justice.

The second year I spent at the University differed very little from the first, but the third brought happy changes. To begin with, I moved from Fourteenth Street to Chancelor Street where Miss Mildred Nelson Page was kind enough to offer me a room in her house. It was a large and comfortable room with a long bookcase which I soon managed to fill. Here, in pleasant surroundings, I could have worked even more than I did in the preceding years, no noise ever disturbing me; yet I can think of no period of my life when I did as little as I did then. The reason was that I had, by that time, made a few friends who often succeeded in persuading me to leave my books either to go with them on a hike through the woods or to spend an afternoon at the moving pictures. I suppose that the Jefferson, our favorite theater, is still standing on the Main Street of Charlottesville, but I fear that it has been "modernized" and has lost much of its character. In 1920, the music was provided by a pianist whose efforts to please were praiseworthy and noisily appreciated by the students; the latter covered the tinkling sounds with roars and stamping whenever they recognized a popular tune, and I can never hear the opening bars of *Suwanee* without being carried straight back to the Jefferson of my twentieth year and hearing that pretty piece of music vigorously accompanied by hundreds of well-trained feet.

The movies were then in their teens, but with their

many ludicrous shortcomings they exerted a peculiar fascination on me. It is strange how innocent we students were, in spite of the fact that we thought ourselves so thoroughly aware of anything ridiculous. We sat through such tedious pictures as *The Four Horsemen of the Apocalypse* and had an excellent time of it.

I now studied little, except around examinations. This, I imagine, was a reaction against the excessive seriousness of earlier years. Strange new books fell into my hands, notably the works of Havelock Ellis which I read with astonished eyes; his stark view of humanity was one of those necessary shocks which help us to grow up and I closed the last volume disillusioned but, I considered, wiser.

By way of earning my living or at least learning to do so (I had asked my uncle to reduce my allowance), I had applied for a post of assistant professor of French, which I was given at the beginning of my last year at the University. On a September morning in 1921, I overcame my shyness after an appalling struggle and faced my class for the first time. In order to conceal my nervousness, I did my best to seem gruff and intractable but found it difficult to keep up. I called my students' attention to the fact that the first page of the book we were to study contained the French alphabet, adding that that page would not be turned until every one of them had completely mastered it and that, if necessary, the entire term would be spent in accomplishing this purpose. At first, they thought I was joking, but when we came to the letter *u*, they realized to their sorrow that I was in dead earnest. Long did we toil over *u*. I neither raised my voice nor gesticulated, but no Ephraimite was ever so fussy about *shibboleth* as I was about *u*, and many were the Gileadites slaughtered on the banks of Jordan.

At that age, I took unreasonable likes and dislikes to people which I was at great pains to conceal; in consequence, I found it extremely difficult to be fair to all the students in my class; but being troubled by my conscience for my partiality, I was unnecessarily pleasant to those from whom I inwardly shrank and showed my favorites as stern a countenance as I could. Be that as it may, we all got along very well together and I flatter myself that if a few Americans know how to pronounce the French *u* correctly, some of them owe this to me.

By the spring of 1922, I had become so homesick for Paris that I decided not to stay at the University another year, as I should have done had I wanted to obtain a degree. I argued that, considering I was going to live in France, I would not need a degree from an American university, whatever profession I chose to exercise. Also, it was high time that I began to earn my living. Moreover, I had a suspicion that my appalling deficiency in Mathematics might bring me to grief at final examinations, but this I kept to myself. My uncle was easily convinced by the arguments I set forth and allowed me to leave at the end of the spring term.

Having made up my mind to sail in the early part of July, I immediately began to examine the drawbacks of my decision. Of course, the very thought of seeing France again made my heart beat faster, but the place I was about to leave seemed all of a sudden immensely attractive for many reasons. It was a beautiful place full of pleasant people. Also, I was going to leave it and that, curiously

215

enough, made it doubly attractive in my eyes. I wished that in some way a part of me might remain in America while another part returned to Paris, and strange to say that is what happened, our wildest prayers being sometimes answered. My life at the University was no longer a lonely one; I had friends, excellent friends whom I have kept. I realized that a tie existed between the University and me, that I owed much to her and that, without being aware of it, I had grown very fond of her. It was pleasant to sit in the Rotunda when the snow was thick on the ground and read *King Lear* or the *Faery Queen*. It was pleasant to walk in the moonlight on the lawn, at the time when the wisteria begins to bloom, and to talk with friends. It was pleasant indeed — but this I realized too late — to be twenty at the University of Virginia. Before I had actually left the country, I began regretting that I had not snatched at what fate had offered and stayed on another year.

My sister Anne had come over in May to pay our relatives a visit and we were to go back to France together. One of her reasons for undertaking such a long trip was that she was anxious to see The Lawn, our grandfather's house in Virginia. It was arranged that she would first come to see me at the University and from there take the train to Haymarket, in Prince William County, where one of my cousins would meet her. Miss Page had kindly invited her to spend a few days at her house and given her a room next to mine. On the day before Anne was to go to The Lawn, we received word, at five in the morning, that the house had been completely destroyed by fire during the night. It was strange to think that so many years had elapsed in which she might have visited the place, and that only a few hours before she expected to see it at last, a flame darting its tongue out of an overheated furnace had sent the house up in smoke.

We sailed from New York on the *Rochambeau* and reached Havre towards the middle of July. An extraordinary elation took hold of me when I saw the shores of France, a feeling so deep and so powerful that one might have thought I had feared that country had disappeared under the waters. As we traveled from Havre to Paris, I was amazed at the beauty of the Norman country side, in spite of the fact that I was already quite familiar with it; what struck me most, I remember, was the impression of great youthfulness which the old province gave me; it looked now, I felt sure, as fresh and verdant as it did to the eyes of the invading Rollo when he swept down the Seine in the tenth century. In this I saw evidence of the perennial strength of France. Wars could wound her, but she always rose again; she was like the sower in the Psalm, who weeps as he goes forth and comes back rejoicing, with his sheaves over his arm.

The suburbs of Paris and the Gare Saint Lazare seemed rather bleak after the glory of the Norman fields, but had they been ten times filthier, I would have loved them just the same. And then to hear French spoken everywhere in the noisy station made me wonder if I was not dreaming; I realized that I had longed so desperately for Paris that I had never left it in spirit, because I was a part of it just as it was a part of me.

My father, Mary and Lucy were waiting for us at 16 rue Cortambert, but I was too overjoyed to say much. Nothing had changed around me. This might have been July 1919 instead of July 1922, and I thought that I would be able to take up life exactly where I had left it then, to go back to the Louvre and wander through the old streets again. I soon found out, however, that three years did make a difference. Going from room to room, I repeated to myself: "This is home. I am home." I went to my room and sat down. The window was half open and I heard two women talking quietly in the courtyard, and this was as it was before, but the room itself looked darker and smaller than I remembered, and there was a kind of eerie stillness in the house. It was strange not to hear the voice of students laughing and shouting. With a sort of leap of the imagination, I saw myself walking down West Range towards the end of the afternoon, stopping to watch the shadows of the trees on the lawn. A sudden wave of

218

sadness swept over me, and I felt irritated with myself for this unexpected change of mind. Did I really know what I wanted? No. I had never known. I was in a constant state of perplexity, wishing I were where I could not be. How, I asked myself, could I ever face life and fight that much talked of battle if I did not even know my own mind?

An American friend of mine came to see me a few days later and, in the course of conversation, asked me bluntly what I was going to do for a living. I stood aghast and could not answer. Of course I had often wondered what I would do later on, but I had never asked myself the question in just this way. It was my theory to let tomorrow look out for itself, so long as today was all right. There was a reason for this, which I did not care to examine too closely, a strange reason which even today I find difficult to explain. The necessity of earning money was abhorrent to me. I liked work, but I did not feel that the work I was fitted for could in any way prove remunerative. The urge to write was very strong in me, as it had been since my seventeenth or eighteenth year, and yet, even in my wildest dreams, I could not imagine that I would earn my daily bread with my pen. Nevertheless I was convinced that I could not be anything else but a writer, but where the money would come from which would keep me alive and enable me to write my books, I did not know; neither did I worry about it. Certainly there was no connection in my mind between writing books and making money; I simply did not believe that I could write books which a great number of people might want to read; I did not even think that any publisher might be tempted to print my stuff. This was not humility on my part; I should rather say it was a form of youthful pride combined with an almost inconceivable bashfulness. "To be great is to be misunderstood," I naively repeated to myself. "I shall be misunderstood. And my books will be published posthumously . . ."

These thoughts gave me strange comfort, but they were of little practical value. Needless to say, I imparted them to no one and preserved a sphinx-like silence when asked if I had any plans for the future. Several hours a day I locked myself up in my room and wrote about everything that happened to go through my mind: poems, plays and essays were begun and thrown aside. To write more than three consecutive pages was not then within my power. I very soon tired of the subject I had chosen and broached a new one which I considered more attractive, until that one too palled on me and I had to think of something else to write about. Curiously enough I was not discouraged by so many setbacks and always embarked on a new piece of writing with considerable enthusiasm and enormous self-confidence. "Today," I thought, "I shall begin to work in earnest. What I have done so far does not count, but now I am about to write something which will make future generations stare!" But as evening grew near and I read what I had written, I was overcome with a sense of failure; it was always a shock to me to see what a flimsy connection there was between what I had planned and what I had achieved. Words would not obey me; they betrayed my meaning at almost every sentence and little by little drew me away from the theme which I originally had in mind. And the future generations had to wait. On the following day, however, I was back at my desk with new plans in my head and a sheet of foolscap in front of me.

That summer went slowly by. We did not go to the country, but Paris in August is anything but unpleasant and I was quite content to remain there. Friends were constantly coming to see us, one of them in particular, whom I shall call Henri, spending most of the day and a good part of the evening with us. We had known him ever since the days of our childhood and were all very fond of him. A gifted, versatile young man, he could do practically anything from designing a house to making a hat. Moreover, his conversation would send us into fits of laughter and time flew when he was about. His gaiety and exquisite sense of mimicry, together with an amazing knowledge of art and architecture and a passionate interest in the French society which Marcel Proust had studied, made him so fascinating in my eyes that I regretted ever missing a word of what he had to say. He was an unusual mixture of seriousness and frivolity. It was impossible to be solemn with him, as everything seemed to lead up to a joke or to one of those stories which only a Parisian can tell in three or four sentences. On the other hand, anyone could see that he was in dead earnest when it came to what he considered his business, which happened to be sculpture.

His father was well off and allowed him to live pretty much as he chose, all the more since the old gentleman lived in Bremen. Henri had a studio near the Place Denfert-Rochereau, but he professed himself perpetually dissatisfied with his work and, like the hero of Balzac's *Chef d'Oeuvre Inconnu,* never allowed anyone to catch the smallest glimpse of what he did. I, however, was better treated than most for the simple reason that he asked me to pose for him. I sat nervously on a straw-bottomed chair, afraid to move or to say anything flattering or otherwise about his work, lest he should immediately destroy it because I had made the very statement which he considered unbearable. Nevertheless, I could not help secretly admiring the excellent quality of his work, the strength and boldness with which the features were treated, to say nothing of a sort of uncanny intuition of his model's character. Like every real artist, he was something of a mind reader and this came out in the best portrait I have ever seen of myself. I was at once amused and a little horrified as everything which I had sought to hold secret seemed to appear in broad daylight. But I comforted myself with the thought that what I read in the portrait could as easily be read, or not at all, in my own face. Two or three more sittings were required. One morning, I received a telephone call from Henri. "Don't bother about coming today," he said. "I've smashed the head to pieces . . . No, I don't think it was very good." And never again was the portrait mentioned.

I was at an age when one is most impressed by a certain form of polished cynicism; at heart I revolted against it, but I admired the qualities that went with it: quickness of mind, wit, infallible good taste and an utter scorn for anything approaching sentiment. There were, however, many things about Henri which I failed to understand. It took little intuition to guess that he was not happy. His gaiety was superficial, something left over from better years. He dreaded being alone and yet the company of most people was insufferable to him. Far too well-bred to be a snob himself, he lived in a world of snobs whom he ridiculed and adored; far too fastidious to be pleased with anything he or any one else did, he was nevertheless capable of childlike outbursts of enthusiasm for some well recognized masterpiece. He was neurotic with a certain freshness of mind and heart, a complicated person with a longing for simplicity. As far as I know, his attitude towards religion was one of complete indifference and he was apparently of the opinion that pleasure alone deserved

223

to be taken seriously. Of his work, he never spoke.

Only after several years did I realize what kind of influence he had had on me, a slight, secret influence such as a person who was so little interested in me could exercise, but of course he was never aware of this. He seldom paid attention to anything I said except, occasionally, to laugh at me; yet I learned a great deal by listening to his conversation. He taught me to distinguish the sham from the real in painting and, far more important than anything else, he unwittingly taught me not to judge myself complacently or to consider that what I did would last forever. His paralyzing self-criticism caused him to throw away the gifts he had received, and this too was a lesson to me: I understood that no creative work could be achieved where too much was expected by the creator and that imperfections had to be taken for granted. Extreme humility and extreme pride are equally negative in art; both blind us to what we are actually capable of doing, and I had a sad example of this in our friend's failure to express himself with the means that were his.

Of course, I realized none of this at the time. If a tragedy was being enacted under my eyes, I was not aware of it. Most lives are tragedies. What keeps them from appearing so is the merrymaking that goes with it all, the joking, the daily chit-chat, the interest in minute events, in one word all that fate does to pull the wool over our

eyes. The gay young man I saw every day with new stories
to tell, new ideas for hats and dresses, was anything but a
tragic figure and would have laughed himself ill at the
thought that anyone could take him seriously, yet no
prophet was needed to foresee what years of sadness and
disillusion lay ahead of him.

Towards the end of that summer, my father asked me
in his quiet reasonable voice if I had any idea as to what I
wanted to do. "You are now twenty-two," he added as if
he were talking to himself. He did not say, as many fathers
would have done: "At your age I was already in business."
Or, "What do you expect to do for a living? When are
you going to start working?" That was not his manner.
For the space of one half-minute, I wildly agitated the
question in my mind, then I answered: "I am going to
be a painter." "A painter," he repeated with polite interest.
"Then you must begin taking lessons. Hadn't you better
ask Henri for advice?"

I did, not without blushing; it is always a little trying
to tell a fastidious artist, who believes that Da Vinci alone
knew how to draw, that one wishes to be an artist. But
contrary to what I had expected, Henri did not even smile.
"Go to the Grande-Chaumière," he said.

The Grande-Chaumière was a fair sized atelier in the
street of the same name, only a stone's throw from the

famous Rotonde. I bought myself a green cardboard folder, some *papier Ingres*, a couple of black pencils, and on a morning in October nerved myself into entering the atelier. The room was full of people and, much to my relief, no one paid the slightest attention to me. I sat down and got my things ready. There was a naked woman sitting on a platform where everybody could see her, and although I thought her extremely plain I drew her as carefully as I could. It was strange how quickly one felt at ease in the atelier. Everybody worked hard and the sound of the pencils on the paper was the only thing to be heard with the exception of an occasional whisper. At the end of thirty minutes, the model got up and stretched. Then she sat down in another position, and I made another sketch of her bony shoulders, large hips and heavy ankles. By the time I got up to leave, I felt like a well seasoned *rapin* and strolled back to the subway with quite a different view of the world.

That evening, my father took me with him to pay a call on his friends the Steins who lived in the next street. Mr. Stein, Gertrude Stein's brother, knew much about modern art and owned a collection of paintings by Matisse who was then achieving almost universal fame. "My boy is going to study painting," said my father as he introduced me. Oh, I wished he hadn't said that! Not in a drawing room full of modern paintings which I was supposed to admire

226

and did not know how to! Particularly terrifying was a lady with coal-like eyes and half of her face painted a bright apple green; nevertheless, there was something fascinating about her expression, half whimsical, half cruel, and the gay angle at which her funny 1905 hat was cocked.

"That's Madame Matisse," said Mr. Stein, who saw I was looking at the picture. "Nice, isn't she?"

He then told me that a gentleman, upon seeing this portrait in Matisse's studio, had asked the artist why he had painted the lady's face green. Whereupon Matisse gave the inquirer a piercing look and icily replied: "Monsieur, her face is *not* green."

My quarrel with Matisse was not that he had painted a lady's face green; Italian Primitives had done so before him. No, what distressed me was that I knew in my bones that I could never paint like him and that I had no desire even to try, although (I fancied) I would be expected to express myself more or less in the same language. "Look at me," the lady seemed to say. "Forget about la Belle Ferronière and her silly smooth cheeks. My face is crooked and half of it is green, and my nose well to one side as if I were sniffing at something. My blind eyes will not follow you around the room in the customary way, because I don't care whether you are in the room or not, but you will never forget me. I am crazy. I am the lady who sticks a long hat pin in her hat, zzzzzz! through the brain! I am modern,

227

mon garçon. I am modern art, and you will come to me some day."

"Well," I thought, as I went home that evening, "there you are. You have decided to be an artist in 1922, and in 1922 artists draw like Matisse who is undoubtedly a great painter, or like Picasso, who may be the Giotto of his century. You thought apples were round, but apples are really shaped like diamonds and you must draw them accordingly."

So the next day, when I went back to the Grande-Chaumière and a naked lady sat down on the platform to be drawn, I gave her a rectangular head and rectangular hips. This was a depressing piece of work. Where curves are reasonably to be expected, I prefer curves and am not ashamed of saying so. Having therefore examined my drawing, I took my India rubber and erased one angle after another, neatly filling up the lines as I went along.

Henri, who also attended the Grande-Chaumière and happened to be there that morning, gave my sketch a glance and said nothing, although I fancied I saw his lips forming the dreaded word "*rondouillard*" as he saw the result of my efforts. Cubism was rampant in those days and anything like a rounded line was looked on with a sneer; this was a source of worry to me, because I could not train my eye to see people as an ensemble of articulated blocks. I suffered from a secret hankering after Greek art and in my heart of hearts placed Scopas and Praxiteles above any artist for the simple reason that they expressed to perfection my own ideal of beauty. This of course was a sin not to be confessed at a time when art was going wild and the "*fauves*" were roaring in art dealers' shops.

I have often thought that I would have been a different human being if, by some dispensation, I had never laid eyes on a Greek statue. A great many thoughts which lay dormant in me would probably not have awakened to life. The whole history of mankind repeats itself in most of us. We all go through a prehistoric age and medieval times; some of us develop into renaissance men and women; not all of us reach modern times and it is only too clear to me that the greater part of humanity is at present still floundering in the dark ages. One nation at least puts me in mind of fourth century barbarians with highly perfected weapons in their hands. Be that as it may, I was just crawling out of what I might call my Gothic period when I first looked at a Greek statue, with other eyes than the eyes of childhood, and I felt at once conquered by an overpowering love of beauty. I felt very much the way a fifteenth century student must have felt upon first viewing an antique torso freshly discovered in a ploughman's field, and I now dimly understood what the Fathers of the Church meant when they said that the gods and goddesses of Greece and Rome were devils exacting worship in the guise

of superhuman beings. I was no more than a pagan returning to his sylvan deities.

All of which, I realized as I proceeded with my *rondouillard* sketch, could in no way be approved by the lady with
the green face. She, I felt, would gladly have poked her
umbrella through Mona Lisa's eye and with the same
weapon have broken to small pieces the lovely collection
of Greek terracottas in the Louvre. Yet, in my mind, she
reigned supreme over modern art. I could see beauty in her
wicked face, but not the kind of beauty which I wished to
express, and here was a troublesome problem: did I have
anything worth saying with a pencil? What I drew looked
like what I might have drawn had I been living at the time
of Prudhon and David, so what good to me were Daumier,
Cézanne and Matisse, all of whom I admired rather indiscriminately? Wasn't it rather absurd to go back when
everyone was frantically rushing forward?

Months went by without helping me to solve my difficulties. I labored over my drawings and achieved some
progress without ever turning out anything which might
even remotely have put one in mind of modern art. I was
so conscious of this that I amused myself by putting fancy
dates at the bottom of my sketches, like January 1810, or
September 1822. I don't think I ever reached 1900. "Ac-
ademic" would probably have been the word used by a
critic, had he been allowed to examine my work, but I was

230

careful not to show anyone what I did; above all, I took great pains to conceal my sketch-book from the fastidious Henri, who might have killed any ambition I had with a smile and a deadly remark.

I was a great walker in those days. On the first of the month, my father would give me fifty francs which I spent as a rule within the following twenty-four hours; the rest of the time I was quite penniless and therefore compelled to walk wherever I wanted to go. This did not bother me in the least. I was so very fond of the streets of Paris that I never tired of roaming from one to another, stopping at shop-windows or peering through open doorways into the mysterious courtyards of the sixth and seventh "arrondissements." The houses in the rue de Lille, in the rue du Bac, in the rue de Varenne filled me with wonder and I quickly familiarized myself with the history of each of them as it is given in the Marquis de Rochegude's excellent guide book. Very often, with this book in my hand, I would go up a dark staircase, past the terrifying gaze of a suspicious concierge, and go looking for a faded fresco on a wall or some bit of old woodwork which my author recommended. In this way I learned a great deal about a city the beauty of which appeared almost inexhaustible. Foreigners who drive through Paris from one museum to another do not realize what they are missing; no one who has never loafed or *wasted his time* in a city can pretend to know it, and Paris, for some reason, is probably as difficult to fathom as any city in the world. Of course, anyone can go there and see what there is to see, from the Louvre to the Moulin-Rouge, but within the limits of Paris exists another city as unattainable as Timbuktu was in former times, not a sacred city but a secret one, one not to be found even in the books which boast of telling us what is not told in the guide books.

This city, which is the real Paris, is taken for granted by Parisians and is therefore little described except by novelists and poets who have lived there, but of course what they know can be conveyed into words only up to a certain point; they can tell you what a little café looks like inside and out, but it would take the uncanny genius of a Marcel Proust to make one understand what it feels like to be in such a place on a bleak January afternoon, for instance, to describe the charm of ugly surroundings, the friendliness of inanimate objects, of the palm with its atrocious red bow, of the torn leather seats and the coarse white marble tables with their black oil cloth writing pads and shabby red penholders side by side with a pale blue bottle of fizzy water, just as we might see them in a still life by Picasso or

233

Derain. And in a certain respect, this is Paris. Everything in the city has an indefinable quality which allows one to say without hesitation, "This is Paris," even if it is only a milk can hanging on a door-knob, or a heavy brown broom noisily sweeping the leaves on a sidewalk, or a row of weather-worn books in a dusty box on the quays. Why it is so I cannot tell, but the city has put its mark on everything that belongs to her. Tourists are too absent-minded or in too great a hurry to notice this, bu. a Parisian's heart will beat at the memory of a flower-pot on a window-sill or of a song whistled by a butcher boy on his bicycle, if that Parisian happens to be far from home. Show him the picture of a baker's shop with a child eating a *croissant*, or the picture of a table and chair on a sidewalk and a waiter standing by with a white napkin under his arm, and he will think, "This is neither Toulouse, nor Lyon, nor Marseille, although a superficial observer might believe so; this is Paris. Good or bad, what comes out of the hands of Paris is Paris, a letter, a piece of bread, a pair of shoes, or a poem. What we have to give to the world is not borrowed, it is our own and can be stolen from us, but not imitated."

At this point, I feel that some will think that I am going too far, that Paris, after all, is a great international city like London or Vienna. Perhaps I can make my meaning clearer by telling of a moving picture which I saw in the States some years ago. It was an American picture about Paris and, sure enough, there was the Opéra and there were the Boulevards, rather hastily shown in order to create what is now called atmosphere. Then we were taken to a café and I began to groan inwardly, for although everything seemed right, almost everything was wrong: the waiters' aprons were too short, and outside the café a policeman walked up and down with a cap which was a trifle too high in the crown, and a goatee like Napoleon the Third's. Because of these little slips — and there were many others — nothing in the café looked like the real thing. This, I thought, is Hollywood, but it is not Paris.

I have always felt proud of Paris, because Paris is my home town. Each walk I took through its streets seemed to create a new tie which bound me to its very stones. I have seen pictures of this city painted by American artists and some of them are extremely pleasing, but I cannot help thinking that it takes a Frenchman to give a really good *likeness* of the place. Landscapes of the Seine and Notre-Dame or the Louvre are accurate enough when painted by foreigners, but they do not and can not convey the same impression as landscapes painted by such Frenchmen as Marquet, or in earlier days by Monet and Daumier. Nor can I explain in what way they differ. Cocteau tells the story of a very gifted Japanese photographer who took a picture of Paris and showed it proudly to his Parisian friends; in the foreground of the picture was the limb of a

235

peach tree in full bloom, which made the whole thing look thoroughly Japanese.

When I was in my twenties, it irked me to hear tourists from other countries talk about Paris, because I felt that they saw the place through foreign eyes and not, I thought, as it really was — that is, as I saw it. I was very intolerant on the subject. I spoke of Paris a little as if I had planned and designed it and as if it belonged to me. When I took my American friends for tremendous walks from Passy to the Gare de Lyon or from Notre-Dame to the Opéra, I felt humiliated if they showed the slightest signs of weariness and no longer looked at the old houses I pointed out; it was like telling about one's love affairs and suddenly realizing that intense boredom is greeting these confidences.

I was particularly fond of walking at night along the river, from the Pont d'Iéna whose naked horsemen stare blindly at the stars, to the Pont-Neuf with its long row of stone masks making faces at the dirty water. I don't know why it is that walking helps one to think, but my mind was never so active as in my wanderings from quay to quay. Imaginary conversations with distant friends occupied me for hours at a stretch, or imaginary letters in which I set forth my plans and theories about everything under the sun: love, art, religion — these subjects were ever new and exciting to me and I agitated them ceaselessly in my brain.

236

I was dazzled by my silly thoughts and felt that I was discovering new worlds. One night, as I was watching the water from the Pont-Royal, I suddenly thought: "Damn the Grande-Chaumière! I am a writer!"

This was like an explosion opening up new quarries. In a second I remodeled my whole life; I could hear the sound of beautiful sentences winding up unwritten stories, I thought of titles as startling as a flash of lightning, I imagined people discussing my books and writing about them. All this was very pleasing and, as the French say, it cost nothing. So I raced home in order to begin my first book without more delay.

It was past midnight when I reached the rue Cortambert and everybody had gone to bed. I poured myself a glass of wine and immediately sat down at the dining-room table with a sheet of foolscap and a pen. Not a sound was to be heard, it was a solemn moment. However, as I scrawled a few disconnected words on the paper "defended by its own whiteness," as Mallarmé once wrote, I realized with sorrow that I had nothing to say. Or perhaps — I comforted myself with this thought — perhaps I had too many things to say; anyway they refused to take shape. No masterpiece came forth, and the fine sentences which I had turned over in my mind on the banks of the Seine sounded suspiciously like tosh once written down in black and white; moreover, it was impossible to find a meaning to them or, if I did try

to force a meaning into these inspired words, it was so trite
that I might more profitably have gone to bed than deliver
myself of such platitudes.

So here I was at the same point as six months ago when
I locked myself up in my room to write my posthumous
works. This was a little discouraging. "I am getting on," I
thought, "I am twenty-three. At twenty-three, Rimbaud
had written most of his verse." Now, for the first time, I
began reflecting that my father was old, that he had retired
from business, and that I had no prospect whatever of earning my living if I did not learn some kind of trade. However, I was such an optimist at heart that I felt certain everything would be all right some day and that I would not
have to go into business.

The next day I stayed at home instead of going to the
Grande-Chaumière, and in the afternoon I took a walk. No
one ever asked me any questions and I did pretty much as I
pleased. It occurred to me that I might be a very good poet
and I sat down on a bench to write a sonnet, but the rhymes
got dreadfully in the way of my meaning, and this occupation was soon abandoned.

Many weeks went by during which I did little else than
draw small pictures of imaginary scenes or write impres-
sionistic descriptions of music and famous paintings; this
I easily coaxed my good-natured conscience into believing
was work. Once in a while, my father would ask me how

238

my work was getting on. "Beautifully," I answered. And
that settled it. I was not in the least worried as to where all
this would lead. There was a tendency in me to see good
omens everywhere. A friend of ours gave me a seventeenth
century book on the title page of which was a ship with
banners flying and sails bulging in the wind; just above
the topmast were written two words which filled me with
confidence and which I immediately adopted as a sort of
secret motto: *"Dominus providebit."* There was something so prosperous and so triumphant about the ship that
merely to look at her made me feel elated, as if, in some
way, she had been my own.

During the winter of 1922-23, I met various people
more or less interested in literature and art, all of them intensely modern in their talk. They had read books which I
had never read and admired things which I considered hideous, but I liked them although their taste horrified me a
little. Once a week, we met at a friend's house where everything that was new in the world of painting and writing
was passionately discussed. This friend, Mr. Rollo Myers,
was the nephew of Frederic Myers, the founder of the Society for Psychical Research and the author of a book which
I had read many times from cover to cover: *Human Personality and its Survival of Bodily Death.* This, I thought,
this at least was a link between me and the light-eyed Englishman whose admiration went to Joyce, Schönberg and

239

Fernand Léger. He was a quiet man with agreeable manners and a subtle sense of humor which never made itself obtrusive; his auburn moustache was not thick enough, however, to hide a mysteriously ironical smile which swiftly came and went when an opinion was expressed which he considered old-fashioned, or bourgeois, or worse: *pompier*. His interest was mainly in modern music; he himself played the cello part in trios or quartets and, although he played Franck and occasionally Schumann, I knew that he was far more attracted by Eric Satie and Darius Milhaud. One day I imprudently asked him why he never played Bach. "Bach," he repeated with the shadow of a smile, "of course; there are some very fine pieces for cello. . . . Perhaps you would care to hear one." Whereupon he sat down and, after looking through a stack of music, finally opened an album and began to play. A more serious face I never saw as he drew his bow over the strings, neither have I ever heard a more repetitious and more uniformly severe piece of music; it made no more effort to please than the multiplication table, and in a way it reminded one of the multiplication table, the austere beauty of which no one would dream of denying, although few but specialists and prigs could pretend to enjoy it. During the first three or four minutes I went through all the stages of boredom and irritation, but finally resigned myself and listened without stirring to a number of *da capos* some of which, I am certain, were not indicated in the score. At last, just as I was wondering whether or not I should lose my mind, the cellist put down his bow and asked me quietly if I had liked the piece. I said that I could listen to that kind of music all day. He threw me a quick glance and agreed that one could never tire of such marvelous stuff; then he closed his album, "and in the book that day we read no more."

Among the people I met at his house was a young man whom I shall call Brochot, a smart, disdainful little fellow with large horn-rimmed spectacles and very definite ideas as to what was worth while and what was not in the world of letters. His manner was a strange and studied mixture of amiability and impertinence, and I don't think any one could say ruder things in more courteous tones. Being extremely quick-witted, he could dismiss almost any problem with a well-rounded epigram, and I dreaded to hear him mention the revered names of Hugo and Balzac for fear of the horrible literary blasphemies that might follow. Someone told me he had actually spoken to Jean Cocteau and this impressed me beyond words, because, although I had never read a line of Cocteau's, I knew that he stood for everything that was clever and modern, and rather wicked. Occasionally, Brochot would announce with a slight, condescending toss of the head that he would read us a poem; then, drawing a paper from his coat pocket, he would begin in a cold, quiet, indifferent voice to tell us the story of a lady who died and went up to heaven in an elevator.

It made me uncomfortable to listen to Brochot. Everyone in the room seemed to think that what he wrote was excellent, but I was at a loss to know what I thought on the subject. Obviously I could never write in the same vein. I believed that words were beautiful in themselves, that they should be used lovingly, not kicked about like worthless old tools; I believed that the aim of literature was to create an impression of beauty even in describing what was not beautiful, and that a book written in order to demonstrate solely the author's cleverness might just as well not have been written. No beauty could I find in Brochot's poems, but I was not quite sure that I understood them. Perhaps there was beauty in jargon, after all, perhaps my ideas on art were old-fashioned. Certainly I thought that art for art's sake was the only possible creed for an artist of any period, but what indeed was art and what was not? In some curious way, my love of Greek sculpture had pervaded my literary taste and I was more and more attracted to classical beauty in writing. This, I realize, is more easily stated than explained. There was a secret relationship in my mind between the face of the Hermes at Olympia and the structure of a fine piece of French prose; it was in the power of both to convey the same impression of serenity and a sort of divine aloofness; yet this did not imply a lack of warmth:

242

I insisted, on the contrary, that enthusiasm was indispensable if beauty was to be created. But, I reflected, perhaps these cold and matter-of-fact writers of the present time have invented a new kind of beauty which I am yet too blind to appreciate. I don't care for their choice of adjectives, and their sentences sound like ill-worded telegrams, but how do I know that I am not wrong?

So disquieted was I by Brochot's lucubrations that I began wondering whether I could be a writer myself and whether I had not been cursed by the lady with the green face. Surely she would have beamed on Brochot and his curious French, but I had nothing to say to which this new Mona Lisa might care to listen. However, I could not judge modern literature by the poems of a writer whose works had not even been printed, I must familiarize myself with Giraudoux and Morand whose names were constantly being mentioned. So I borrowed Giraudoux's *Suzanne et le Pacifique* from a public library and began reading it, not without a certain feeling of uneasiness because I could not rid myself of the idea that my future as a writer depended on my ability to speak the same language as this brilliant exponent of modern style.

At first, I was dazzled. The terseness of each sentence, the bold choice of similes, the dry wit, the exquisite words, everything about the book seemed faultless to me; it was like listening to a conversation between people who were infinitely cleverer than I — but what were they talking about? Not ten pages had I read before I realized with considerable dismay that I could not even make out what the subject of this novel might be. I went on more attentively, but the further I advanced the thicker grew the darkness around me. Surely a novel must have a plot, even a modern novel. So I looked for the plot and could not find it. Talk there was, a lot of it and of the very best quality too, although it was as difficult to follow as a discussion on *Tao*, but no real action that I could see and not a trace of sentiment. That was what struck me as more disconcerting than anything else: these characters were all brain. To be sure, they were amorous at times, but even then their lack of feeling was almost monstrous: they were like dissipated Martians. I put down the book with sadness and wondered more and more about myself.

What puzzled me was that the urge to write stories should be so great in me in spite of my fruitless efforts to produce more than six or seven pages. This I did not dare confide to anyone — it was too painful — but I hinted darkly at a tremendously long novel the material for which I was slowly gathering. Even Brochot was a little impressed. "Are you going to give your book to the N.R.F.?" he asked. I said I would think it over. "Of course you couldn't think of giving it to any other publishing house," he went on, "unless perhaps you have a mind to give it to Grasset."

I said that the matter demanded consideration. These cryptic and slightly disdainful answers made me go up in Brochot's estimation. He was a kind fellow at heart and much of his nonchalance was merely put on. I saw clearly that he did not know what to make of me but he did give me the benefit of the doubt.

Some time later, he invited me to come to see him. He lived in a small room near the Place Denfert-Rochereau and had asked a few friends to meet me. Parisians are always curious to see new faces, and it was not long before the divan was crowded and most of the guests seated on the floor. There was a little of everything among them: medical students, bank clerks with literary ambitions, painters on the look out for a gallery to exhibit their work, all of them gay and somewhat coarse and cynical. They were so talkative that it was impossible to hear the sound of one's own voice, but having little to say I was only too pleased to hear others hold forth, and listened in complete silence to the expounding of crazy theories and to scandalous tales about well-known people. There was nothing repressed about Brochot's guests, but I in the midst of them felt like a mass of inhibitions (to use the language of the time). One of the more reserved among these was a blue-eyed Spaniard called Pruna. He was Picasso's only pupil, I was told, and painted agreeable pictures of monumental women in classical attitudes; his delicate sense of color and the charm

245

of his well-behaved drawing were already making him popular with certain picture dealers who felt that cubism was in its last throes. We all looked up to him and Robert Lefort, a loud-mouthed, flashy boy who was studying chemistry, called him a genius to his face.

This Robert Lefort with his brilliant, nonsensical talk and his superior way of referring to Proust as Marcel and to Cocteau as Jean, impressed me more than anyone at Brochot's because, although he was younger than I by one year, he seemed to have read, seen and experienced everything under the sun. "Mon cher," he once told me condescendingly, "you and I are good for nothing. I am twenty-two, you are twenty-three, and we haven't produced anything. It's too late now. Life is over." He was inordinately proud of his looks and made himself insupportable by his sarcastic remarks and indiscreet questioning; his quips wounded the sensitive; yet he was often invited and when he wasn't invited he came just the same. His ringing voice damned this and praised that with almost unbelievable peremptoriness, but even skeptical Brochot considered him a sort of oracle; it was impossible to discuss with him without being ignominiously roared down or mortally stabbed in one's pride with a poisonous word. He made me feel clumsy and ignorant, but I unwillingly admired him, and I believe that, in spite of his horrible faults, most of us found it difficult not to like him, for the same reason that

246

people liked Steerforth, who was a bully of the same kind.

One of us, however, stood up to him and talked back every time, a young Jew called Morhange with a shrewd gray eye and a long, straight, intellectual nose. He was absolutely impervious to Lefort's charm and answered him in a flat measured voice which put one in mind of a steel blade feeling for the right spot. He was imbued with Lenin's ideas on the remodeling of our world and vented them boldly; there was something coldly passionate about him which attracted as much as it repelled; intelligence was written all over his narrow face. Politeness and simplicity characterized his manner, but when provoked by Lefort on some ticklish subject he would immediately flare up in the most surprising way and, without raising his voice, kill as it were, his adversary with logic. I remember that, one day, after a ruthless argument in which Lefort was badly beaten, Morhange gave him a piercing look and with slow and studied emphasis recited these lines from *Athalie*:

> *Le cruel Dieu des Juifs l'emporte aussi sur toi.*
> *Je te plains de tomber dans ses mains redoutables,*
> *Ma fille . . .*

Discussions of this kind I found very stimulating. So great was my desire to write that almost everything I saw or heard served as an incentive in that direction and I soon formed the habit of keeping full notes of whatever struck me during the day, a street scene, a face, a sentence; but how to make use of all this material was still a mystery which I had not fathomed. I painstakingly described people I had seen and derived some pleasure from these observations, but although scraps of writing accumulated in my drawer (which I kept locked), still they were only disconnected sketches and could by no means be called a book. Nevertheless they kept me busy at my desk, and in spite of the fact that they did not seem to lead me anywhere, I could not feel that I was altogether wasting my time.

When I look back on those days, particularly in the light of recent events in France, I can think of them only as a time of great happiness. To be sure I had worries, but it took very little to fill my heart with joy, and constant lack of funds did not seem in the least to interfere with my pleasures. For the sum of two francs and with the tickets at reduced prices which we were sent from time to time, I was able to find a seat in the top row of the Opéra, from which vertiginous heights I listened spellbound to the *Walküre* or *Boris Godounov*. Or I would stand in line at the old Gaieté Lyrique until I was finally admitted to that part of the theater which the French call the hen-roost or sometimes "le Paradis." However, I did not care how much I had to climb so long as I was allowed to see *L'Oiseau de Feu, Mercure* (a seldom given ballet by Eric Satie and Picasso), and *Parade*.

248

Before the present war, one occasionally came across old bores who would buttonhole you, when Russian ballets were mentioned, and say: "Ah, but if you had seen Nijinsky! . . ." No doubt they were right, but I would not care to sound like these *"laudatores temporis acti"* by saying that the ballets were far better in 1923 than they are at the present time. Yet nothing can be truer. Many believe that the ballets died with Diaghilev. I do not think so; they survived him by a few years with considerable brilliance, but the lack of a guiding genius is now telling on them and has been for some time. Be that as it may, we who have seen the curtain rise on a Russian ballet in the early twenties, witnessed something which the present generation cannot very easily imagine. To begin with, that mysterious element which people call atmosphere was totally different. The wild excitement which preceded the show created an almost unbelievable tenseness in the house as well as back of the stage. Cocteau has admirably described the scenes that went on between the producers and the dancers and also the nervousness of the public. Drama was perpetually in the air. Rumors spread that the drops were not ready, that so and so refused to appear because his costume was wrong, or that some members of the orchestra had decided to go on strike at the last moment because typewriters had been introduced as musical instruments; among the public, gentlemen were ready to fly at each other's throats at the least provocation, having already taken sides before even one bar of the score had been played, and one could always count on a lady or two fainting during the performance. The names of Satie, Picasso and Matisse meant war in those happy days, a harmless if vociferous war with no blood drawn except from a few angry noses.

The battle of *Parade* is too famous to be described again. I was not present on the first night, when the Comtesse de Pourtalès rose in her box and, her tiara all awry on her gray head, waved her fan and exclaimed that she had never been so insulted in her life, but I did hear a storm of disapproving whistles, hisses and cat-calls drown Eric Satie's music. What drove the opponents of modern art to a frenzy of disapproval was the appearance of a man carrying on his shoulders a landscape of skyscrapers and chimney pots; why this should have nettled them so is hard to explain, unless it was because it came as a finishing touch to something they had borne too long. Thunderous applause from the other half of the audience strove to silence the noisy opposition, and between its admirers and its detractors, the music fared as it could.

Of course there were lulls. I remember a hush of admiration when Leonid Massine appeared in *Mercure* as the messenger of the gods. This great creative artist was then hailed as the best dancer alive in spite of the growing fame of Serge Lifar whose sudden appearance in *La Chatte* sent

250

electricity through the house; something like a nervous commotion seemed to shake the very air we breathed; it was as if we had fallen under a strange, almost diabolical spell; the stage was bathed in a sort of phosphorescent beauty which brought to mind Baudelaire's haunting allusions to a mysterious other world of dream and splendor. So powerful was this impression that some Catholic writers expressed the view that the devil had a hand in the show, and indeed it is not difficult to see what they meant.

I came home exhausted and with a head swimming in music. If this was the modern world, Heaven bless the lady with the green face! I too would be modern. Far too agitated to sleep, I sat down and wrote delirious accounts of what I had just seen. Never before had life seemed more exciting, more beautiful. It was impossible that I should be left out of all this, that I should not have something to say in the brand new Paris that was awakening. I went to bed reluctantly with a feeling that sleep was a waste of time when I had books to write. For it always came back to the same thing: I wanted to be a writer.

On an afternoon in June 1924, I received a visit from Morhange. He had never come to see me before and I wondered
what could have brought him. First he embarked on his
favorite subject: Lenin. I listened in silence, neither demur-
ring nor yet agreeing with anything he said, except when
Morhange asked me if I had noticed that Lenin had Shake-
speare's brow. I could not controvert this fact which seemed
obvious enough. Then followed anecdotes on Lenin's wit,
on his kindness to the oppressed, on his pertinacity in right-
ing even a very small wrong. There was something so gross-
ly subtle about the means employed by my visitor to con-
vert me to Communism that I felt like laughing in his face.
All of a sudden, he was seized with a sort of prophetic fit
and painted a picture of the future of Europe under Communist rule, which, he said, was as unescapable as the re-
ceding of the coast along the Channel. He had a kind of
self-conscious eloquence together with a curious sense of

252

style which made his sentences rather pleasing; not only did his words have color, but they also seemed to have a shape and a weight of their own; the strange thing was that, having been put together with some degree of ability, they produced an effect of drabness, or perhaps the subject itself lacked the picturesque quality which would have rendered it attractive in my eyes.

Quickly passing from one mood to another, Morhange informed me that he was about to launch an *avant-garde* magazine which was to be called *Philosophies*. "Philosophies in the plural," he added with a significant look. "We are averse to no special form of thinking, so long as it is alive," he explained. "*Philosophies* is not sectarian."

"I suppose it is Communistic nevertheless," I said.

"We have Jean Cocteau among our collaborators. Would you call him a Communist?"

"Why, no."

"Max Jacob is also sending us something. Is he a Communist?"

"He is a Catholic."

Morhange opened his hands as if to say: "You see!"

"But," he went on, "I am also founding another magazine of a different type. I shall call it *La Revue des Pamphlétaires*. Nobody in France has written any pamphlet worth reading since Paul-Louis Courrier. I want to revive this essential form of literature, I want to make it something living and aggressive and dangerous, something that will start trouble."

"Start trouble?"

"I mean something that will set people thinking. People are apt to go to sleep nowadays, Green. We must shake them by the shoulder. Do you ever read our Prophets? Are you familiar with Amos, with the opening chapter of Isaiah?"

He proceeded to quote some of the most violent denunciations of those great Jews, all the more skillfully since he knew how interested I was in the Old Testament. Then, in a quieter tone of voice, he asked me if I wouldn't care to write the first number of this new magazine. "The whole number?" I asked.

"Why, yes. You can do it. Write thirty or forty pages. Attack something or someone. Have you no grievances?" he asked as he saw a bewildered look on my face. "Can it be that you manage to live without some kind of grievance?"

"Oh, I have plenty of grievances! For one thing, I don't like Catholics."

"No more do I. An excellent theme for a pamphlet."

"But I am a Catholic."

He was quick to see the possibilities of the situation.

"Your position is all the stronger," he said. "You can murder the whole lot of them in the name of faith."

254

He enlarged on this at length, with the talent of his race for seeing all sides of a problem at once, and here was a problem which he held up to my intellectual gaze like a many faceted diamond. It was very characteristic of him to throw himself into a state of cold and gratuitous enthusiasm about a question which left him, at heart, completely indifferent; in the same way, he could have worked himself into an artificial frenzy over medicine or algebra; but what was real in him, apart from a longing to overturn the capitalistic world, was a delight in juggling with ideas, a sort of atavistic hankering after a higher form of Jewish *jeu d'esprit.*

I needed no encouragement of this kind, however; the thought of writing a pamphlet against Catholics had never entered my brain before that minute, but I saw in this a means of expressing much that lay dormant in me. Had I gone deeper into this matter, I would have understood that it was not so much what I had against Catholics which I wanted to put into words as what I had against myself as a Catholic. Although I do not intend to give a detailed account of my religious beliefs at the time, I find it impossible not to touch lightly on the subject in order to make my position clear. Since the age of fifteen, when I became a Catholic, I had gone through all the phases of zeal and lukewarmness familiar to so many; only indifference had I never experienced. Periods of daily attendance at mass alternated

255

with longer periods when I stopped going to church altogether, this from a keen sense of contradiction between
what I believed and what I did; but despite these fluctua-
tions, my confidence in the Church remained what it always had been. There were times when, having entered a
church, I came out almost immediately thinking: "This
is hypocrisy." On reflection, such an attitude showed more
pride than humility of spirit, for what are churches to be
filled with if not with sinners?

Be that as it may, I began writing my pamphlet directly
Morhange had left the house. Words flowed from my pen
with a facility which I had never experienced before. It was
as if whole sentences had been waiting in readiness somewhere at the back of my mind. I wrote slowly but never
stopped until I had covered three large sheets of foolscap,
and went to bed that evening with a strange feeling of
peace; this indeed was the first time that I had unburdened
my mind of a load which it had carried for years without
suspecting it. On the following day I proceeded with my
work, and within the better part of a week had brought
this little book to a close.

Having typed my MS., I sent it to Morhange with little hope of receiving a favorable reply, for, I argued, how
could a Communist Jew care for a book so deeply concerned
with religious problems and a book which, moreover, had
so little to do with our times? Nevertheless, it was an en-

couraging thought that I had been able to carry out a plan and produce something which at least had a beginning and, thank goodness, an end.

Next day's mail brought me a note from Morhange acknowledging the pamphlet which he said he had examined and was prepared to have printed. I read this communication with mixed feelings. On the one hand, it was intoxicating to think that some printers were actually going to set up my words which eventually would find their way to the public; but the fact that Morhange refrained from expressing any opinion on my work made me blush with mortification. This, I thought, was my reward for laying open my secret to the gaze of an unbeliever, and with much bitterness of spirit, I remembered the words of Scripture: "*Secretum meum mihi.*"

That very afternoon, however, I was handed a *pneumatique* from my unbeliever. He explained that his first impression of the book had been one of surprise, owing to the unexpected bareness of its style, but that a second and more attentive reading had reassured him. What followed made me wonder whether he was not poking fun at me and I could not believe that what I had written deserved such praise; yet, I reflected, no Jew would accept and print such a book and run the risk of making a fool of himself for the sake of pleasing a Catholic; it must be that he liked it.

Our next meeting convinced me that he was serious

257

enough; several matters were discussed, principally that of the title, and *Pamphlet contre les Catholiques de France* was agreed upon as best describing the book. Then a pseudonym had to be found, because the thought of seeing my name in print was no less than horrifying to me, particularly on the cover of a book which contained so much that was personal; I would rather have made a public confession of my most carefully hidden sins than tell an unknown reader about my private views of religion. This, I thought, was my legitimate secret; I considered it irksome enough that one person should know it, and that person a man totally unsympathetic with my point of view. So I cudgeled my brain and finally produced the clumsy and improbable name of Théophile Delaporte.

Only one question was not discussed by Morhange and me, a delicate question yet a question so *terre à terre* as to make a poet shudder, a question which I cannot say I evaded because it did not enter my mind that it could be agitated, one which Morhange was tactful enough not to bring up, so that our sensibilities were spared: I mean royalties. Apparently there were no royalties, and if there was any virtue in my book, virtue was to be its own — and only — reward. I had never had money dealings with anyone in my life and was absolutely unprepared to cope with a problem of this sort; in fact, many months went by before it occurred to me that I should normally have been richer by a few hundred franc bills on the day my pamphlet appeared; but I did nothing about it.

The book came out in October 1924, a thin, square book with a pale blue cover which had little to attract attention except a band of flaming red paper around it with these words printed in bold letters (Morhange's idea): *Dédié aux Cardinaux Français.*

Of course I could not resist telling my family that I had written a book and presented each of my sisters with a copy of it. My father too was given a copy, but he was a little puzzled by its contents. "Why," he asked Anne, "is the fellow so enraged at Catholics? How does he want them to live? Like birds, in trees?" Being a Catholic himself, I suppose he was nettled by my ferocious upbraidings.

A number of articles were written about my pamphlet at the time of its appearance, partly, I think, because of its frenzied disregard of actuality and the oddity of its theme. It was not very long before the book was out of print, but it was not republished; neither was this first number of *La Revue des Pamphlétaires* ever followed by a second. I had apparently killed the magazine.

One day in November 1924, I was, very much against my will, taken to a literary afternoon. I had promised to go some time before, but when the hour actually came for me to put on my hat and wend my way, I was seized with a powerful desire to stay at home. To face a drawing room full of writers seemed to me almost as awful as jumping into the bears' den at the Jardin des Plantes, and I suppose that there is a relationship between a literary drawing room in any country and a bears' den, the fundamental difference being, in my eyes, that bears are more straightforward in their methods.

A few minutes after five, I found myself in an exquisitely furnished parlor the windows of which faced the majestic Dôme des Invalides. Luckily I had arrived as one of the most illustrious French poets of the day was holding forth in a circle of spell-bound admirers, and I had no trouble in slinking into a corner where no one could notice me. The poet was a small woman with a dead white skin, heavy black hair and enormous black eyes which sparkled with excitement; there was a strange and unconventional beauty in her face which put one in mind of Pallas Athena, but in her less fortunate moments she had a look of Pallas Athena's owl. In any case, her features had a bird-like cast which made Cocteau compare her to a swallow. Something in her manner struck me as odd: she had a peculiar and rather unlovely way of throwing back her shoulders and thrusting out her stomach, her elbows close to her waist and her arms at right angles with her body. Her voice was clear and sharp; it never paused but slowed down ever so little at the fall of sentences as if to gather new strength. Probably because of Cocteau's remark about her face, it occurred to me that this woman's voice might be compared to a swallow's flight with a sudden swooping down to the ground and a quick rising up again to new heights. No person had ever been known to succeed in stopping her when she had decided to make her point; she listened to questions and contradictions with ill-concealed impatience and once more her voice rang out in the stuffy drawing room. Her name was Anna de Noailles. She had written much which younger authors considered old-fashioned, but some lines of hers seemed to stand a fair chance of lasting as long as the language. When, at the end of a heated monologue on politics, she looked around with a glint of victory in her eyes, I and several other people were introduced to her but I doubt that she even saw us as she was like a Delphian priestess coming out of a trance.

There were many more writers whose names have not all succeeded in finding their way into the public's memory, playwrights, poets, critics, journalists, anxious to come to the fore and have their say, to shine, as the French have it. In a corner of the room, standing with an elbow on the edge of a piano and a look of disgust on his face, was Mauriac the novelist. His long bony face, his grin of disdain when things were mentioned which he did not like, his garrulousness and sudden fits of ill-temper, his Bordeaux accent, his provincial mannerisms, everything about him made one think: "This can't be Mauriac, this must be one

261

of Mauriac's characters." However, this impression was merely superficial, and a closer acquaintance with the Catholic writer allowed one to discover another and strangely fascinating person: an ugly man who said that he was the ugliest man he had ever looked at, a backbiter who tore himself to pieces with far deadlier ferociousness than he tore at others, a scoffer who scoffed at Mauriac, an old student ever ready to join frivolous demonstrations in the Latin Quarter, and at the same time a Catholic as serious as any reformer, a good friend and a poor enemy, a cynic, a tease, a pitiless fault-finder, impatient, intolerant, irascible, unkind in his judgments, unfair in his likes and dislikes, pleased only when he felt that he displeased someone, yet so brilliant and so amusing, so generous at times and at all times so forgetful of wrongs that he had suffered, so quick to take up for a friend, so easily conquered by fine sentiments, so fond of danger although danger frightened him, so totally lacking in wordly prudence, so irresponsible and so human that one found it almost impossible not to love him.

How I wish that I had kept a diary at the time instead of contenting myself with jotting down "impressions" of things and people! It would be interesting now to know what was said that afternoon and, since the talk was mostly political, what prophecies were made, if any, concerning the future of the nation. Nor would it have been beside the

262

point to note, as I did in later years, casual opinions and off hand judgments which, although inconsequential in 1924, would nevertheless have faithfully given the tone of the period. No matter how dull an entry in a diary may seem to the writer on the day he makes it, years will give it an ever increasing interest; but to realize the truth of this requires an effort of the imagination for which few people are prepared, and thus much valuable material, the very texture of our life and times, is forever and absolutely lost.

That day, in that same room, I made a friend whose friendship has never failed me, nor do I need a diary to call this event to mind. We have been together through good and evil days and I write his name with affection: Robert de Saint Jean.

CHAPTER ELEVEN

Among the unfinished stories which filled my desk-drawer, there was one to which I added half a page or so from time to time, simply because I was anxious to know what would happen to the characters. Then no more than now could I make a draught of a plot, as writers are supposed to do before they embark on a book. My method was to begin to tell the story and make it up as I went along, much in the fashion of a nurse who tells children stories at bedtime. However, the nurse's aim is to put her audience to sleep, whereas it might be thought that I wanted to give my readers insomnia.

The story bore the title of *The Pilgrim on the Earth* (taken from Hebrews 11.13). It started out more or less like an autobiography (with the exception of the prologue which was written last), and only little by little did the supernatural element creep into it. As I went on, I got farther and farther away from my own actual experience as a student at the University of Virginia and watched with

264

interest the picture becoming darker and weirder; it was like losing one's way in a wood and realizing by slow degrees that the wood is haunted. I suppose there is no harm in admitting that I was frightened, particularly on one occasion when I understood that I was describing a case of what theologians call possession. This came as a shock, yet acted as an incentive, for I now wrote large portions of the story at one sitting and kept up at this pace until I had actually reached the conclusion.

It was a proud moment when I was at last able to write the word *fin* at the end of my first story, and I could hardly believe that I had really completed a piece of fiction. What worried me now was a question of such a curious nature that I hesitate to mention it. Did my book really *sound* like a book when read aloud? What I meant by that I no longer know very well, except that I wondered whether I had produced something formless which no publisher would accept. I was at times painfully conscious of the fact that I did not write like the more successful novelists of my day, in that dazzling, elliptic style enriched with new images. What I had to say, I said in a bare, direct way and with not the slightest desire to flatter my reader's taste. It seemed only too probable that people wouldn't care for this sort of thing.

In my perplexity, I consulted a friend whose experience of literary matters was already great in spite of the fact that he was my senior only by a few years. Jacques de Lacretelle is now one of France's best known authors and a member of the French Academy. In 1924, he had written a short novel about a Jew which had received enthusiastic applause from the critics as well as an important reward. He wrote in an extremely polished style, the effect of his sentences being that of a beautifully glazed surface in which objects and faces were reflected in a clear and faithful outline. One of the qualities I admired most in him was a deep-rooted love of the French language which he knew certainly much better than many writers of his generation. Words fascinated him; he thought of them, it seems to me, as people with a long family history, hard-working people whose fortunes had known ups and downs. I am greatly indebted to him for introducing me to that great masterpiece of learning and beauty, Littré's *Dictionary of the French Language*, which I have studied for many years without exhausting its vast resources.

It was very trying to have to hand my MS to a writer so fastidious in his likes and dislikes, so profoundly attracted to classical literature that his very choice of words might have been approved by Marivaux, whereas what I had written — I realized it the very instant I gave him my story — was wildly romantic. Whatever he thought of the story, he was too well-behaved and tactful a man to point out those of its shortcomings which were inherent in the

266

author's mind, and his answer was one which I have not forgotten: he himself took the MS to his publisher, Gaston Gallimard.

Apart from having published the whole of Proust and many works by Gide, Cocteau, Morand and others whose names were synonymous with success, Gallimard owned the most important literary magazine of France, the *Nouvelle Revue Française*. He was particularly interested in discovering young authors, whose works he accepted, I think, rather indiscriminately, his reasoning, I suppose, being that quantities of MSS would of necessity yield a certain percentage of literature. I was not aware of this when, a few weeks later, a letter signed by Gallimard himself informed me that he had decided to publish my story in book form as well as in his magazine, and would I care to pay him a visit in order to discuss terms with him. To discuss terms with Gallimard! Would I care? . . . My head swam.

The following afternoon, I was sitting in one of those large, comfortable armchairs which are supposed to put a man at a disadvantage by making him feel too much at his ease (or so authors say who have sat in them — my future publisher had no such thought, of course!) and across the table from me sat Gaston Gallimard, a short man with a benevolent pink face and masses of white hair which contrasted with the childlike expression of the pale blue eyes; his shirt was a bright blue, his manner simple and cordial.

He knew that I was interested in painting and told me how his father, who was celebrated for his fine collection of Renoirs, used to take the precious canvases out of their frames when he considered they needed a good cleaning, then lay them flat on the floor and brush them with a broom dipped in soap and water. After a few minutes' talk during which we exchanged opinions on modern art, Gallimard handed me a contract which, he said, had been prepared for me, and would I kindly read it. It was beautifully printed in italics on a fine cream colored paper, but I had never read a contract in my life and, although the words in this one were familiar enough, they made little sense to me. However, I took it for granted that such a handsome document was unimpeachable. At the end of five minutes, I was asked if I had any alterations to suggest and I looked as important as I could and said no. Then it might be a good idea to sign this paper now, might it not?

I agreed. Two copies of the contract were then signed and countersigned; one was tucked away in Gallimard's desk drawer, the other I folded and slipped in my pocket. Only when I had shaken hands with my publisher and taken leave of him did I realize that precious little had been said about my story, but I was far too happy to worry about such a trifle.

It pleases me to think that my first story was inscribed

to Robert de Saint Jean. He and I had so much in common
that, although we had met only recently, I sometimes had
a vague impression that we had been brought up together
and that we had forgotten about it in some unaccountable
way. There was only a slight difference in age between us,
he being younger than I by ten months, and what surprised us most was that, in a city where we had so many
friends in common, our paths should not have crossed
earlier. Robert's outlook on life had great similarities with
my own. He had been released from military obligations
two years before and was undecided as to what he would
do, but his natural bent was towards literature. Diffidence
prevented him from publishing anything he had written
and he was too modest to perceive in himself the qualities
which he so much admired in others. The very few pieces
of writing which he allowed me to see convinced me that
his desire for literary perfection would hamper him as long
as he did not decide to take a plunge like the rest of us.
He wrote exquisite French and possessed to an eminent
degree that gift of his race for choosing the right words in
order to express the subtlest feelings. I envied him this
quality. It seemed to me that as soon as I took pen in hand,
I revelled in the obscure: that is, I had a tendency to make
the obscure appear more obscure, whereas Robert could
throw light on a subject without depriving it of its mystery or, as the case might be, of its charm. Although he

269

never criticized me as often as I wished — this in spite of many entreaties — I can truly say that there are very few Frenchmen to whom I owe more in the matter of clarifying what I have to say. For some reason, I have always found it extremely difficult to change what I have written, but in writing my novels I have always had it at the back of my mind that I was telling Robert a story and this has helped me more than I probably realized at the time.

We went out often together, one of our main pleasures being to attend the Lamoureux concerts at the Salle Gaveau. As a rule, we sat in what we considered the best seats, as high up as one could go. We waited in silence amid the buzz of conversations, then the lights were dimmed and in the hush that ensued came the moment to which we had looked forward for a whole week. There is something unforgettable about the stillness which precedes the opening bars of a great piece of music, a sort of nervous expectation which can be met only by the powerful voice of the orchestra. It was delightful and at the same time almost unbearable to wait and wait in the dark, sometimes for ten or fifteen seconds, then all of a sudden to feel one's self freed as it were by the magnificent roar of a Beethoven symphony. With beating hearts, we listened to many works of overwhelming beauty. How keenly we felt that our enthusiasm was allowing this music to become a part of ourselves! But it was useless to try to express it;

we were stunned into silence. I have often wished that I could hear the *Eroica* once more *for the first time*, for now the days are gone when I could listen to it and hear it; by that I do not mean that I have gone deaf, but that I am too familiar with it to listen with anything but a dispassionate sort of admiration to this boisterous masterpiece. And so it is with much music, ancient and modern, of which I thought that I would never tire.

There are many reasons for liking music at the age of twenty-five, one of mine being that in a curious way it inspired me with extraordinary self-confidence. I suppose that few men with any degree of ambition can listen to great music and not be stirred in their hearts by a longing for greatness. That is what music does to you: a few chords will raise you to an almost superhuman plane where everything seems within your grasp, love, happiness and glory. As I sat listening to Schubert or Debussy, I imagined strange and beautiful books coming out of my brain, sentences the like of which no one had ever read; I felt like a man drunk with hashish revelling in heavenly delusions of grandeur; but mine was a wide-awake dream, I actually put together mentally the opening words of a new book, snatches of dialogue went through my mind. When the music stopped, however, this blissful state came abruptly to an end and there only remained an acute longing for the great unwritten masterpieces. I knew only too well

271

from bitter experience that as soon as I put pen to paper my words would look like the poor relatives of those I had envisioned.

One of the most curious problems a writer has to solve is how to produce beauty with the words which he uses to discuss the most trivial matters of everyday life. Music has a privileged position; yet forty or fifty men must get together to play a symphony, after much rehearsing. Painting and sculpturing necessitate tools, colors, canvases, clay, stone, to say nothing of certain conditions of space and lighting. The approach to these arts is neither simple nor direct, whereas a writer, I mean a born writer, could actually write anywhere with the stub of a pencil, on a piece of dirty paper; neither marble nor paint, nor music, is the means which he has at his disposal to express himself, but the very language which he uses in a shop where he buys a pair of shoes or in an office where he is compelled to thrash out a money matter with a business man. The stuff his books are made of is of necessity a coarse material. Nothing can be more hackneyed than most of the words his dictionary has to offer, yet these words placed in a certain order produce a sonnet by Baudelaire (who used the tritest of words with the greatest effect), or, placed in another order, an advertisement for a new kind of hair oil. There was to me something very compelling in this thought. I knew that great painters succeeded in making the quietest tones

272

stand out as vividly as bright orange by carefully planning their color scheme, and there was no reason why the same should not be done with words, if words could be thought of as something like thousands of little touches of color like the dots in a painting by Seurat.

With some hazy idea of this kind at the back of my mind, I began writing a novel about three misers. There was nothing beautiful about the subject, the characters were dull and rather sinister people, and the story was told in the simplest language, with such a paucity of adjectives that any one might have thought that I had never read a book except the *Code Napoléon* so highly recommended by Stendhal. My ambition was then to tell my story without ever allowing the reader to be diverted by the style in which it was written, a sort of invisible style, good and strong, if possible, but not in any way noticeable. This complete effacement of the author seemed to me one of the major requirements of literary perfection. I wished to make it impossible for my reader to know what kind of man had written the book — a curious desire, I allow, but I was possessed with the idea that the characters should speak and act for themselves and never be interfered with by the author's personality; in order to adhere more strictly to this theory, I made my characters as unlike myself as possible.

Robert, who was my only confidant in these matters,

listened with a sympathetic ear and did not contradict; he thought, I imagine, that theories concerning books matter very little so long as the books themselves are worth reading. I had moments of despondency when the imperfections in my novels made me long to throw the book aside, but, although he had not read a line of it, Robert urged me to go on with the story, and so great was my confidence in his judgment that I did keep on.

Since the early part of winter, I had been saving my pennies in order to be able to pay my share of a trip which Robert and I were planning to take during the summer holidays. A china apple was the receptacle for the one and two franc pieces which I contrived to put aside by dint of walking instead of riding in the bus, and it was really amazing how rapidly my hoard increased, but I suspect that extra coins were slipped in by my father when I was out. Once in a while, I fetched a knife and worried the money out of the china apple: after long efforts on my part, one piece would come out, then all of a sudden five or six in rapid succession, then more and more until the table seemed to be covered with brass francs. Yet there weren't enough to take me very far; I might perhaps, with what I had, have gone to Orléans and back, but we had planned to spend a month in Auvergne and another month in the Pyrenees. Finally I decided to sell a book which Robert had given me and which I have never ceased to regret, a

274

copy of *Les Plaisirs et les Jours* by Marcel Proust with illustrations by Madeleine Lemaire; I was given fifty francs for it by Mr. Rossignol, a dealer in second-hand books whose shop was one in a series of many in the rue Bonaparte. Today, the rue Bonaparte seems almost as far in space as those happy years do in time, but the very name of Rossignol brings certain memories so vividly to my mind that I can almost see the rows of calf-bound books in their cases and the huge green portfolios bulging with prints in a corner of the somber shop where a gas jet had to be lit, in winter, as early as three in the afternoon. Portly Mr. Rossignol examined Madeleine Lemaire's drawings with a look of professional indifference and handed me a fifty franc bill.

What with this money, Robert's, a hundred francs which my father gave me and the contents of the china apple, we had managed by June to scrape together a sum which seemed enormous to me but which could not have exceeded four hundred francs; we did not need any more, and all we had to do now was to wait for the holidays.

Robert was then assistant editor of a small but very popular magazine called the *Revue Hebdomadaire* which we nicknamed the Revue des Dromadaires because of the large number of old ladies among its faithful subscribers. Many famous writers had contributed to this magazine, the size and shape of which was much like the *Reader's*

Digest: Maurice Barrès, Pierre Loti, Paul Bourget, and in later times Jacques Bainville, François Mauriac, Montherlant; even Jean Cocteau had sent in essays, stories and poems. The office of the editor was located in the courtyard of one of the finest of old Parisian *hôtels,* the Hôtel de Sourdéac, one part of which was occupied by Plon, the publisher.

It was impossible for Robert to leave before the twelfth of July and there was nothing to do but to be patient. I had not been to the country since 1915 (unless one could think of going to Argonne as going to the country) and struck off the days on a calendar in my desire to see them hurry by. Would that they could be given back to me now and properly enjoyed; I was as happy then as I have ever been in my life; but a week, or a month or even a year of happiness seemed nothing out of the ordinary and I don't think it ever occurred to me that this state of things could come to an end. Yet I remember that a shadow was cast over those bright days by certain events, the meaning of which I was not capable of fully grasping at the time.

Alexandre Millerand had been ousted from the Presidency by a combination of forces which later were to unite under the general name of *Cartel des Gauches:* this was an alliance of the Leftist parties against the Rightist tendencies of the Chamber of Deputies. In a way, the *Cartel des Gauches* was a forerunner of the *Front Populaire.* I need not go into this matter further except to say that the access to power of the Left Wing caused deep unrest in all parts of France. It was instinctively felt that the *Cartel des Gauches* was not lucky for the country. Money behaved as it always does when the Left gains the upper hand in politics: it rushed to the borders, so true is the saying that in France the heart is on the left and the pocketbook on the right side.

Communist agitation grew bolder and bolder, particularly in what is known as the red belt of Paris: that is, the suburbs where so many factories were so unwisely built at the beginning of the century. There were demonstrations, much singing of the *Internationale* and much waving of the red flag. People were killed in clashes with the police and the more combustible of rightist or conservative papers like *L'Action Française* or *La Liberté* were loud in announcing a revolution such as the country had never seen.

The dread of a revolution is one of the many nightmares which France has had to live through ever since the distant days when anarchists began tossing their bombs, towards the middle of the gay nineties. *Le grand coup de balai*: that is, the general sweeping up, was the name given to this bogey which actually never came. It was whispered in bourgeois circles that there were Communist cells everywhere, in the department stores, in banks, in all

277

Government buildings, the Préfecture de Police included. Servants were Communist spies, so were concierges. Black lists were ready; somebody knew somebody who had seen them. It was impossible to buy one's self a new hat or a theater ticket without being secretly reported to the cell in charge of one's house. The *Grand Soir* was at hand with its revolutionary tribunals, its commissars and its firing squads not to mention the torture chamber which played an important part in the horror tales about Soviet Russia and Bela Kun's Hungary.

Finally, a date was set by fear for the probable outbreak of the revolution. This precision in prophesying the very hour of a dreaded catastrophe is usually the culmination of panic. For some reason, the twelfth of July was chosen as the last day of bourgeois society. Many people left Paris early that month instead of waiting for the end of the school term. Need I say that the twelfth of July went by as quietly as possible. The fear-mongers were not discouraged, however. They pointed out that, of course, the Communists were waiting for the national holiday to go by and all the bourgeois to leave for the country; then, in an empty Paris, they would proceed with their much talked of *coup de balai;* there could be no opposition and we would speedily have a Soviet government.

In those days, I was even less posted on political matters than I am today and it was difficult for me to judge what real foundation other than fear existed for these rumors. The thought that something might happen to a city I loved more deeply than any city in the world was extremely disturbing to me and I had my small share of the general anxiety. At last came the day on which Robert and I had decided to leave for Auvergne. All worries were brushed aside. We met at the Gare de Lyon and towards evening pulled out of Paris on our way to Issoire in the Puy-de-Dôme. As we caught our last glimpse of the quays along the Seine, the same thought came to both of us: "Shall we ever see this again?" But the exhilaration of going to the country did away with care, and not an hour had passed before we were asleep.

The next morning we were at Issoire where we took the bus that was to carry us to our destination. Up went the bus along the mountain side with the obstinacy of a beetle, nor did it seem to move any faster. Once in a while, it stopped at a village and a peasant woman would climb in with a black handkerchief tied over her head and a large basket full of chickens over her arm, or a cattle-dealer with a cap almost covering his ears and a radical paper sticking out of his pocket.

At the end of an hour, we stopped a few minutes at Saint-Nectaire whose old church stands on the edge of a cliff and watches over the road. We went in. The sun touched the massive pillars as it had done for eight hundred years and allowed us to see the strange and beautiful capitals peopled with crusaders on horses, husbandmen tilling the soil or beating their wives, devils tempting bishops or pestering a saint by blowing out his candle. The church itself, with its mysterious shadows and simple lines, had much that appealed to us both; it is always very moving to find one's self in a place where over twenty generations have prayed and hoped; here more than any-where else, I think, can the pulsations of the country's heart be felt. France herself is ever present in these old churches, France with her dreams of greatness, her sor-rows, and the beauty of her unconquerable soul. I was deeply aware of this and would gladly have lingered at Saint-Nectaire, but we had to be on our way.

Towards noon, we reached a village called Besse-en-Chandesse where rooms had been reserved for us in an old-fashioned hotel; they were very simple but we were quite contented with everything and immediately took a walk through the streets. There is something almost inconceiv-ably ancient about Besse: the dark and rather sinister little church goes back to the year 900, but no date I can give is capable of conveying the impression of immemorial age which the stones of the village walls make on one's mind; they seem almost contemporary with the smooth, rounded mountains and in a strange way they look as if they were a part of them.

As we wandered in the fields and sat on the grass to look at the rows of hills in the distance, I experienced a feeling of extreme happiness which I cannot recall without melancholy. Being studiously inclined we had taken serious books to read, but we found it difficult to concentrate under the triumphant August sky and in a landscape which excelled in beauty anything I had yet seen in this world.

I worked at night. Our rooms were small and so badly lighted that I had to supplement the electricity with the light of several candles which I placed on my writing table, and I have often thought that much of the peculiar atmosphere of this novel (*Avarice House*) was due to the flickering tapers which I used to see by.

We came back to Paris a month later, stayed a few weeks and left again, this time for the Pyrenees where we spent a month in a small town on the Gave de Pau called Saint-Sauveur. From our windows, we could watch the mountain torrent rushing down the poplar-grown valley of Argeles where Charlemagne's armies had passed eleven centuries before. Peasants mowed their fields and shepherd boys played on small Jew's harps as they led their goats up the mountain slopes. No other sound was heard but these eerie little tunes coming from the distance or the swish of the scythes cutting the grass in the field below the house, and the perpetual murmur of the water. Our rooms had white muslin curtains and old-fashioned mahogany furniture. The serious beauty of the valley, the faint smell of verbena which floated in the sunlight, all this comes back to me with a strange vividness and something of a poignancy. We left Saint-Sauveur early in October. A few days before, I had completed my book which I called *Mont-Cinère* after a volcanic lake in the neighborhood of Besse-en-Chandesse.

So I returned to Paris with a full length novel in my bag. It was with a feeling of rather childish pride that I took it out, when I reached home, and laid it on my desk, but I feel bound to explain that its bulk more than its contents impressed me; the important thing in my eyes was that I had succeeded in writing two hundred consecutive pages. Now at last I had won some degree of confidence in my ability to write a book, but whether the book was publishable or not was quite another matter.

Robert had read it with the greatest care. He was to be the first reader of all the novels I have written since and his criticisms have proved invaluable to me. I remember that what bothered me about *Mont-Cinère* was the fact that it so little resembled any type of book that people read in our time, whereas this was precisely what recommended it in Robert's mind. He decided to submit the novel to the editor of the *Revue Hebdomadaire;* I parted

282

reluctantly with my MS and spent the next two or three days in qualms which occasionally changed into wild hopes.

The verdict was reassuring enough. Robert told me that a part of the novel would come out in the magazine and that *Mont-Cinère* was now being read by Messrs. Plon, the publishers, whose offices were located in the same building as the *Revue Hebdomadaire.* A few days went by and I was sent a contract which I signed on Robert's recommendation. I have often wondered what I would have done had he not been there to advise me; business was not my forte, and all I could see in a contract was a rather tiresome piece of jargon, but Robert was very scrupulous in perusing this document and suggested alterations which later proved considerably to my advantage.

We had then reached the end of 1925 and I welcomed the new year with a feeling of buoyancy which I had never known before. I thought of the ship engraved in the frontispiece of my Cassianus, and could not help saying to myself that the wind was beginning to fill the sails, ever so lightly, no doubt, but with a promise of long voyages. It pleased me to identify myself with this ship and to fancy that I was at last under way after having remained at anchor so long.

The N.R.F., as the *Nouvelle Revue Français* was called, had begun to print my story, which was to come out first in the magazine, then in book form in a collection of young authors. Each volume in this collection had a portrait of the author as a frontispiece and I was asked to find an artist who would make a drawing of me; in case I did not succeed, the N.R.F. would designate an artist of its own choice to do the job. This alarmed me somewhat because I had little confidence in publishers' taste; on the other hand, I knew no artist except Pruna, who was away at the time. After giving the matter much thought, I decided to ask Cocteau whose pen drawings of Radiguet, Auric, Picasso and others had a sort of nervous grace, a quickness which put one in mind of Baudelaire's sketches. It so happened that a few weeks before he had sent me his latest book with such a cordial inscription that I did not hesitate to write to him. He knew me only as the author of that strange little book on Catholicism, or thought he did, but we had met two years before at a friend's house where he had talked in a brilliant and frivolous manner about many aspects of literary life with which I was not then familiar. Perhaps he did not care to remember this, although I could not see why. Whether his memory served him or not, however, he wrote me a charming letter saying that he would do his best, but that his hand "did not have wings every day."

I went to see him one evening after dinner. He was then sharing a flat with his mother in the rue d'Anjou, just a block or two from the Madeleine. The house had an air of nineteenth century prosperity which contrasted sharply with my idea of modern poetry; it was difficult to believe that such a bold writer as Cocteau could live in this old-fashioned *décor*. Such were my thoughts as I got into the crimson plush elevator and began pulling on the rope encased in velvet, thus causing the ponderous vehicle to ascend slowly and hesitatingly until we had reached the top floor.

I rang and was shown in. The hall was large and somber; books in mahogany cases gave it an air of bourgeois respectability which I knew well and liked, in spite of its heaviness, because it was a part of French life and went with many valuable qualities; nevertheless I preferred it in other people's houses rather than in our own. Hardly had I taken off my coat when another door opened and I was asked to walk in.

Cocteau was standing in the middle of his room, a small, spare man with almost incredibly bright eyes and a shock of ink black hair which made his face look dead white. He walked up to me with both hands stretched out and immediately began talking. What he said I do not remember, but the words he used were like the words of a language I had never heard before and yet understood perfectly. They were the words which we uttered every day unthinkingly whereas Cocteau seemed to give them a new meaning; trite phrases became beautiful and rare because of the unexpected way in which he placed them in sentences; a poor, commonplace expression suddenly acquired luster and the freshness it had known in its youth. Cocteau's talk was a series of surprises which delighted the mind and kept it in constant expectation of greater pleasures. It was like the speech of an enchanter, one of its effects being to make the listener feel that he was suddenly thinking faster than he had ever thought in his life, and that he was mentally being taken on a journey in a strange new world. As I write this, I realize how woefully inadequate my words must sound in their efforts to describe what escapes description; it is like trying to convey an idea of the flight of a bird to a blind man. Cocteau told a story in three sentences and made it so vivid that years could never efface it from one's memory. Thoughts and feelings almost invariably suggested images to him, similes which no one had ever dreamed of, many of them of a surpassing beauty which made one regret that every word he said could not be taken down. One of the ways he most often began a sentence was: "It is like . . ." (*C'est comme . . .*) followed by delightfully fanciful comparisons which left one breathless; he would then thrust his head lightly to one side, like a bird, as if he were listening for an answer which could never come, and say: "*Quoi?*" *Quoi* did not mean that he expected you to reply — indeed what could one reply? To listen and to hope for more was all one would have thought of doing. With coat sleeves unbuttoned and slightly turned up so as to show most of the cuffs, the poet went on with ever growing excitement, now giving a portrait of Anna de Noailles or Serge de Diaghilev which made you wonder whether they were not actually before your eyes, now explaining in a few inimitable sentences the secret of Rimbaud's genius or describing a street which you fancied you knew well enough and discovered you had never really looked at. The theory that poets are dreamers was constantly given the lie by this wide-awake little man whose precise and exquisite speech seemed ever to be dispelling shadows. I was so astounded that some time went by before I became aware of the aspect of things around me. If the hall was as familiar to me as that of hundreds of French homes, this room was unlike any room I had ever seen.

The bed was an ordinary brass bed with a silk eiderdown on which the pages of a manuscript had been carefully spread out. Here was nothing unusual, but on a long table nearby were a quantity of rare and fascinating objects which so excited my curiosity that I could hardly keep my eyes away from them. Cocteau realized this almost before I did, and with the adroitness of a champion skater cutting figures on ice, drew the conversation to a magnificent crystal globe which he held up in his bony hands. I

287

could find only the simplest words to express my admiration, but these very words he took from me, as it were, and transformed into something almost as transparently beautiful as the very object we were looking at. Such was the gift of this, the most remarkable talker I have ever known: he seemed to create loveliness out of nothing or to enhance it supernaturally where it already existed. Hardly had I examined the crystal globe when a mask made of painted cardboard was placed in my hands, the mask to be worn by one of the actors in Cocteau's adaptation of *Antigone*: it showed a white face with faultlessly regular features and an unforgettable expression of horror obtained by no other means than a slight raising of the arched eyebrows. This was the work of Picasso. There were several other such masks on the table, silently bewailing the fate of the Theban virgin and staring with empty sockets at the ceiling, from which an object of marvelous ingenuity hung and imperceptibly swayed from side to side as we moved around the room.

At first I could not make it out very well: I fancied that I saw a face but directly the thing turned ever so little, it became what looked like a mass of meaningless wires; at another moment, the face reappeared, and watched me with half opened lips, as if about to speak. This wonderful toy, which has since so often been imitated, was made of pipe cleaners twisted and fastened together so as to give the outline of a head and indications of features, the whole thing hanging on a string attached to the ceiling. Most weird were the shadows it cast on the walls as it was made to revolve in the light of a lamp. I believe Cocteau was as proud of this object which he had invented as Leonardo seems to have been of the monstrous playthings with which he used to terrify his friends: lizards with wings, heads of Medusa presented in a mass of writhing serpents. No doubt Leonardo's mysterious personality exerted some influence on Cocteau at this period. Like the great Florentine, the French poet took pleasure in causing surprise, sometimes with an admixture of fright or at least a hint of disturbing elements which added zest to the performance. In this, to be sure, he was in the French tradition, in the tradition of Baudelaire who painted his face green or of the Surréalists who were then beginning to make what they called *des plaisanteries pas drôles* which involved the shedding of tears and sometimes blood.

Finally we came to the business which had brought me and I sat for my picture. Three or four sketches were hastily made and more hastily discarded, until at last one was considered passable by its author and given to me as a present; it was drawn, I remember, with a penholder the wrong end of which was dipped in ink and used as a pen, and of course there was a star in one corner as a signature. How pleased and proud I was of my evening can hardly be

with head well bent, in her bold, absent-minded way.

Anne and Lucy and I were left with my father. The house was quiet and a little sad. Mary's piano still stood in the little parlor but was silent, as none of us played. Sometimes, when I was alone, I would try to strike a chord or pick out a tune with one finger according to the strange method my friend Gilbert had taught me years ago: *"Mon vieux,* it isn't at all difficult and you don't have to bother about learning scales. Just remember the position of the keys in relation to the keyhole. Two whites to the right of the keyhole, then four blacks on the same side, then one white to the left, and so forth, and you have your tune."* This did not take me very far, but I experienced a real pleasure in listening to the sound of the notes, putting my ear as close as I could to the piano in order to hear the reverberation of the strings. How often I had listened as a child to the erratic and disconnected tunes played by our piano tuner, to his proud, mad chords following hesitatingly on each other's heels or stopping all of a sudden as if they had forgotten something and turned back in a somber, distracted mood. All this came back to me as I fumbled on the keyboard, not without a slight wistfulness. My confidence in life was unbounded, but I knew that I had been happy up to this moment, whereas I could not tell for certain what lay ahead of me.

We had now been living ten years in the rue Cortambert

and I had become very attached to our home, yet I realized that it was slowly becoming a part of me and this was not good; then as now, I believed that a sentimental attachment to places is necessarily a limitation to one's freedom, and I wanted to be free, although what this freedom was I could not exactly tell.

Even as late as 1926, I was still such a child that I thought of our flat as the prettiest I had ever seen. The front rooms were bright and gay, and my sister Anne saw to it that there were always flowers in every vase; thanks to her taste in arranging furniture, I believe the two parlors were as pleasing as they could have been. The black rosewood chairs and sofa looked very handsome against the pale yellow wallpaper and the rows of leather-bound books added much to the aspect of the rooms. The dining room, however, with its chocolate-colored walls and its monumental red marble mantelpiece could not be redeemed. It was chocolate-color because all French dining rooms of a certain period were chocolate-color and somehow my father had done nothing about ours when we moved in, but it was a source of worry to Anne and me.

I have already mentioned that my father had retired a year or two before. Being a man of very few words and of anything but a complaining nature, it was impossible to know exactly how he felt about this. On the day he came home and told us that the European branch of the

Southern Cotton Oil Company was to be closed, he smiled as usual and hummed old Civil War tunes, but we realized afterwards how worried and unhappy he must have been. About a week later, he returned from his office in the rue du Louvre with a flat parcel which he put away in a drawer. It was the brass plate which had shone for over twenty years on his office door and which bore his name in thick black letters: Edward M. Green, special agent for Europe of the Southern Cotton Oil Co.

His hair was completely white now but he held himself as straight as ever and took long walks in an effort to fill in the long idle days. A look of great sadness would sometimes come over his features when he thought he was not observed and I knew how keenly he missed my mother, but no word on this subject was ever spoken. Chief among his worries was our future, as he had only just enough money to keep the house going and could not hope to leave us anything. In spite of the fact that I had signed a contract with one of the most reliable publishers in Paris, I don't think he was quite sure that I could earn my living by writing books. Most of his old friends were dead and the only person to whom he dropped a hint of his secret anxiety, strange to say, was the tax-collector, who afterwards told me!

It was not in me to worry, however. My trust in the future was such that one might have thought fate had

294

given me its solemn word to treat me kindly. I knew my
father could not live very much longer — he was seventy-
two and in poor health — and that when he was gone I
could not count on anyone to help me, but the idea was
firmly rooted in me that so long as I wrote now, everything
would be all right later on. I had begun a series of essays on
English literature, which I called *Suite Anglaise* and hoped
to sell at a fairly good price. Anne was very busy too, having
become a regular correspondent for several English and
American magazines.

My first novel, *Mont-Cinère,* appeared in the spring
of that year and was favorably received. I remember that,
a few days after it had come out, I was walking up the
avenue Kléber and stopped near the rue Hamelin, where
Marcel Proust had died, to look at some books in a shop
window; my novel was not among them, but a number of
Les Nouvelles Littéraires lay unfolded on a table and to one
side of the front page, in fairly large letters, I read my
name. It was a shock to me; I felt myself blushing and
walked away quickly. To this day, I cannot tell why I
behaved so strangely. I experienced pleasure mixed with
a sense of shame and did not breathe a word of what I had
seen to anyone, hoping that it would pass unnoticed and
yet wishing that it were noticed. I felt like the old lady in
The House of the Seven Gables who rang a bell and mur-
mured: "Oh, I hope no one heard me!" But Robert soon

came in waving a copy of *Les Nouvelles Littéraires,* and gladly would I have stopped my ears and said: "Don't tell me! I don't want to know." I am not so coy now.

My father read the book and reproached me with a smile for having filled his sister's house with misers. I don't know if I mentioned the fact that I had laid the scene of my story in my aunt's house, in Fauquier County, Virginia. It was a fine old house which General Lee mentions several times in his letters to his son as a place he enjoyed being in, and it certainly deserved better treatment at my hands than to be razed by fire, in the last chapter of my novel.

No one, not even the author, was more pleased with the success of the book than Robert. He had already written an article about my Pamphlet, the first article ever to be written about a work of mine, and he now wrote another on *Mont-Cinère.* Nor was this by any means the limit of his generosity. Only many months later did I learn that he had taken the trouble to write at length to several important critics in order to recommend my story to their attention. One of these critics, Edmond Jaloux, did a great deal to help me on my way and increase the sale of my books. To be sure, there were also articles lacking in amenity, some of which cut me to the quick because I was then ridiculously sensitive, but today I can only say thank goodness there were. What nettled me more than anything

296

was to be told, as I was bluntly told by a few reviewers, that, since I had left love out of this first novel, it was very obvious that I could not treat the subject adequately; they saw in this an admission that I could simply not write about love. I decided to refrain from answering otherwise than with a book which would silence my critics.

About this time, my first story, *Le Voyageur sur la Terre,* began to appear as a serial in the *Nouvelle Revue Française.* After the first installment I had a pleasant surprise. Paulhan, the editor of that magazine, showed me a letter he had received from André Gide asking for the proofs of the second installment of my story, as he did not want to wait a month before knowing how it was going to end. This was so encouraging that I felt like sitting down immediately and starting on a new novel; on second thought, however, I came to the conclusion that it might be wiser to wait and see if I could devise an interesting plot before embarking on a fresh story without knowing what it was going to be about.

Once a week, Robert reviewed books in several literary magazines. Some of these reviews were lengthy and the subject matter so ably handled that they soon called attention to the author's name. One of their greatest qualities was, I think, the sincerity of the feeling which prompted him to write them. He was absolutely unafraid of conse-

quences and said what he had to say with such felicity
of phrase that I made a collection of these articles for their
literary value. He differed from older critics in his desire
to find some good in the books he reviewed, but he could
tear at a frothy novel so savagely that one might have
thought he had been attacked and was defending himself;
this came from an extreme regard for literature, the cause
of which was then being imperiled by a sort of mass pro-
duction of trash. As I have said before, almost any kind
of book could be printed in those days of literary inflation.
Geniuses were being discovered every week by certain publishers who succeeded in ramming dismal imitations of
Morand or Giraudoux down the public's throat, this
operation being made possible only by unheard of pub-
licity such as Balzac himself could hardly have deserved.
This state of things lasted as late as 1931, when the
great depression put an end to one of the worst periods of
cheap literature France had ever known. It is a source of
amazement to look at a publisher's list around 1925: out
of fifty or sixty names, barely two or three survive. Writers
were sent stacks of these books which they sold to second-
hand dealers practically for the weight of the paper.

The serried ranks of geniuses found one of their deadli-
est opponents in Robert, who wrote them up with a pen
dipped in undiluted vitriol. At the time, he was himself
engaged in writing a novel, and it is very much to his

credit that in days when it might have been so easy to have this book printed, he refused to do so, preferring to wait until he had brought it to the greatest point of perfection which he felt capable of attaining. Of this novel he made little mention to me, and many years went by before I was allowed to read it.

That year, we had decided to spend our summer holidays in Alsace, a province neither one of us knew well. What happy days those were when the prospect of spending a month in a quiet little Alsatian village kept me awake at night for sheer excitement! My suitcase, which I had packed and unpacked a number of times, was ready a whole week before the date we had fixed; it was the choice of books, principally, which made it necessary for me to re-arrange the contents of this old-fashioned cowhide valise, a faithful companion of my father's, who had traveled with it from Moscow to Palermo and from Stockholm to Algiers as hotel labels could testify. Finally the longed for day came: on the first of July, Robert and I met at the Gare de l'Est in a blazing sun. As we got into our compartment, I was almost overpowered with a sense of happiness such as I had not known for years; the brightness of my childhood days seemed to have come back to be lived over again.

However, I cannot say that I felt as carefree as I did when my father and mother used to take us to Andrésy and we all shrieked for joy when the train pulled out of the station.

I had a difficult problem to solve and some doubts as to my ability to do so. For several weeks I had been trying to think of a good plot for my new book, but so far had not struck anything which satisfied me, and in moments of despondency I remembered having read somewhere that it was comparatively easy to write a first novel, the real test of a novelist being his second novel. I felt very deeply that I was now expected to show my mettle to those who had seen in *Mont-Cinère* a promise of better books and I was determined, for reasons I have already indicated, that this was to be a love story. Time and again, I had sat down and thought of all the situations that can be brought about by love. This, of course, was the wrong approach: only reminiscences of plays and novels floated up and I wanted desperately to create something new. At last, I made up my mind to dismiss the matter for several days and give it fresh attention in the train. Curiously enough, I expected the motion of the train to act as a sort of stimulant, having noticed that I was never mentally more active than while traveling by rail. What the explanation for this may be, I do not know very well, except that in some obscure way swiftness of motion may be correlated to swiftness of thought, but having seated myself in a corner of the compartment, I now made a new and earnest attempt to construct the plot of the story which I wanted to write. We were to reach Colmar by the middle of that afternoon and I fervently hoped that by dint of will-power I would step out of the train with a new book in my head; but town after town flew by, fields, forests and hills, and nothing came to me which I deemed worthy of being written. My imagination had not helped me in the least.

It now occurred to me that I was losing my way down a blind alley and that I had to come back and view the problem from a different angle. Why did I think a plot necessary? Because I had read that authors invariably made outlines of their novels before writing the first chapter, and this seemed so logical that it sounded like nonsense to controvert it. To be sure, I had written my first novel without knowing very well what it was going to be about, except that my aunt Lucy Turner's house was to play an important part in the story, but it was hardly reasonable to suppose that this lack of method could bring good results a second time.

However, going into the matter a little further, I thought of some of my favorite novels and suddenly realized an interesting fact: I remembered the characters better than the plots; in some cases, I had almost entirely forgotten the plot, whereas the characters stood out with amazing vitality; I knew what they were like and what they were capable of doing, but what actually happened to them had faded from my memory. The adventitious was almost entirely eliminated by an unconscious process of elimination (if I may be excused for using such long words). Actions and utterances remained only inasmuch as they were a part of the character's real self. For example, *"C'est la faute de la fatalité"* was unforgettable because the whole of Charles Bovary's moral person was summed up in this pathetic sentence.

The author creates characters, and the characters create the plot. Strictly speaking, the author should not meddle at all with the plot. The plot is no more his business than a full grown man's private affairs are his old parents' business, and authors, like old parents, usually come to grief when they try to make their spiritual children feel the weight of their authority and fashion their children's lives according to their own ideas. Such was the truth which I was dimly beginning to understand when our train pulled into the Colmar station. I had not found a plot, but I had found something infinitely more valuable.

Our destination was a little town in the foothills of the Vosges called Orbey. A local train took us there and by the end of that afternoon we were unpacking our suitcases in two smallish rooms from which we had a fair view of the mountains. This was well enough, but something bothered us which neither one of us cared to mention because, shocking though it was, it sounded a little futile to take exception to it: the wallpaper. From floor to ceiling, it was covered with large blood-red discs placed at regular inter-

302

vals and encircled by skimpy garlands of daisies which, by contrast, heightened rather than subdued the effect of this strange and sinister decoration.

However, we pretended not to see it. Robert made himself comfortable in an armchair with a book, and I sat down at a small table which I had placed near the window. With a pen, a bottle of ink and a sheet of paper in front of me and no idea of what I was going to write about, I felt for a moment that the urge to write a story was perhaps being defeated in me by a lack of necessary material. Perhaps I had said all I had to say in my first book. There was something devastating in this thought but I struggled with it and finally dismissed it. I remained absolutely still and several minutes went by when something Carlyle was reported to have said on a similar occasion floated through my mind: "I felt as if my head had been filled with mud." It was a curious way of putting it and I played with the idea a little while. If a great man like Carlyle confessed to his inability to write at certain moments, I too was entitled to difficulties of the same kind.

What I regretted most was not having some kind of object in front of me which I might look at in my efforts to concentrate. When I wrote *Mont-Cinère*, my eyes were constantly meeting an old photograph which my father had taken of a drawing room in Savannah, an ugly but picturesque room from which I had derived a kind of inspiration, trying to people it with characters of my own fancy. I traveled with it as I might have traveled with a fetish. But I had no fetish for this second book, although I found one a little later. Presently I found myself thinking of the rue Cortambert. It was a waste of time to think of the rue Cortambert, or so it seemed to me.

The shadows were lengthening on the hills and the only thing I had written on my sheet of paper was the date and, at the very top of the page, "Chapter One." This proved to be of little help. Why I kept going back to our flat in the rue Cortambert, I did not know. I was in the chocolate-colored dining room, the one ugly room in the house, and I stood in front of the "graveyard," a collection of family portraits which hung side by side on the wall by the window. Did other people have "graveyards"? I wondered. In French it would be called *le cimetière*. A *cimetière* on a wall was a curious thing when you thought of it. Dead people watching you, dead people whom you resembled: to this man you owed your eyes, to that woman your expression and perhaps some of your thoughts. It might be possible to use a *cimetière* as a starting point in a novel. No harm in trying. I would describe a *cimetière*, but somebody would have to be looking at it, somebody standing in front of it, not I: a woman.

She was standing in the dining room, looking at the photographs. Her name was Adrienne. I wrote this down.

All of a sudden, I saw Adrienne in my mind's eye as distinctly as if she had been in the room with us. Why she was so absorbed, I could not tell. I knew nothing about her apart from what I saw. She stood still and then someone called her from the next room, her sister. A bit of dialogue followed, a dialogue made up of things people say when they are bored to death; but surely Adrienne was not bored, she was unhappy; at times she had the look of a person under the spell of a hypnotist. And why was her sister so disagreeable to her?

Having written about twenty lines, I laid down my pen and thought: "What can happen to such a character as Adrienne? I must try to think of something exciting."

But I could think of nothing, and yet, the more I concentrated my attention on this girl, the more real she seemed to me. I suddenly became aware that, commonplace though she might appear at first glance, this person was just as mysterious as any human being, and just as much *alone*. She breathed and moved in an atmosphere of solitude which gradually became oppressive. I was not altogether conscious of this. I was too young then to realize that most of us never quite succeed in breaking down the barriers that separate us from the rest of humanity. To be sure, the contacts are manifold and the exchange of thought almost incessant, but no one who is in the least reflective and sensitive can fail to remark how very imperfect this communication between human beings can be. So much is unexpressed, so little can be said. When we are about to speak and reveal something about our inner life, who is in the mood to listen? And should someone be near and ready to heed our words, can we be sure that he understands what we really mean? Words are so clumsy and create such confusion. How many times, having tried to explain, have we sadly given it up and once more retired within ourselves!

Such was the real theme of *Adrienne Mesurat (The Closed Garden)*, and for that matter, the theme of most of the stories I have written since.

The next morning, we were awakened by the sound of sawmills in a nearby factory and immediately decided to leave that very day, but where to go? After lengthy enquiries at the baker's, the tobacconist's and finally the Mairie, we were told of a little inn on the side of a road leading to the Linge, a hill which had seen much hard fighting in the last war. The name of our place of destination was Hautes-Huttes, a strange name considering that the only house at Hautes-Huttes was the inn I mentioned. We arrived there towards the end of the afternoon and were shown to rooms which we thought lovely although they were as simple as the rooms in a peasant's house. Immediately in front of the inn, across the road, lay wheat fields where harvesters were busy with their scythes, and in the distance beyond rose the Vosges mountains. It was as peaceful and beautiful a scene as we could hope for and I lost no time in going on with my book, having first pushed the table as close to the window as I could.

Robert too had brought the first pages of a novel in his suitcase; he worked slowly and said very little about his book, and almost ten years had to go by before he let me read *Le Feu Sacré*, a delightful and moving story which I have mentioned at length in my diary.

The summer went by quietly with the exception of a few days towards the end of July when much emotion was caused by the sudden depreciation of the franc. I mention this because, in the face of subsequent events, this minor catastrophe fades into insignificance. At the time it occurred, we had left Hautes-Huttes which we found a trifle lonely, and had rented rooms in a hotel at Munster, a gay little Alsatian city at the foot of the Vosges. Why the franc should have slumped so suddenly, I can no longer remember, but I have not forgotten the anxiety that ensued. One would have thought that the whole country was tottering on the brink of an abyss. So general was the consternation that we decided to take a day off and go on an excursion. So we got into a bus and went to Turckheim, about twenty-five miles away, where we spent a comparatively happy day looking at the fine old houses and Gothic churches, and when we came back that evening, we read in the afternoon papers that M. Poincaré, *le sauveur du franc*, as he was called a little later, had formed a new cabinet, that the moribund franc had rallied *in extremis*, and that everything was all right once more. O happy days when a crisis meant only a few hours' uncertainty and a slight headache which an aspirin tablet dispelled before you knew it!

Five or six weeks later, we returned to Paris.

CHAPTER   THIRTEEN

To come back to Paris towards the end of a fine afternoon, in late September, when the horse-chestnuts have turned brown and the apartment houses look dark against a bright blue sky. . . . Let me think of it! There are not many people in the streets and quite a few stores are still closed, but Paris is slowly waking up after its long slumber; there is a stimulating coolness in the air; cabs roll up and down the Boulevards, laden with trunks and all kinds of heteroclitous luggage. The holidays are over, but who can feel sad about returning home, when home means Paris?

Nothing could please me more in those days than to jump into a cab, at the Gare de Lyon or at the Gare Saint Lazare, and give the driver my address: 16 rue Cortambert. At home, after the first five minutes of conversation with my father and my sisters, I would go from room to room with an extraordinary feeling of elation. It was as if the very walls and every piece of furniture knew and silently greeted me; they were glad that I was back and I felt sure

309

that I had happy days to spend in their company. The floor
shone like metal, the chair covers were immaculately clean,
the glass on every picture had been washed and rubbed;
there was a faint and pleasing smell of wax and turpentine
in all the rooms. I looked at everything as if I had never
been in the flat before, I looked at the books all carefully
dusted, at our funny rosewood chairs, at the rugs — a little
threadbare, but rugs shouldn't look too new — at the pictures in their old-fashioned frames. Everything was all
right. A long and happy winter was ahead of us, with
plays, concerts, new books to read, new friendships to be
made. Everything was quiet in Paris, everything was all
right in our world. There had been no revolution, after all;
there probably never would be one, and there was, of
course, very little talk of a possible war in those remote days
when the word *nazi* had not yet become a part of our vocab-
ulary.

How safe we felt in the rue Cortambert! Except on Sunday mornings, when people came out of the Protestant
Church, the *temple* as it is called, and out of the convent
chapel facing it, the street was as quiet as any street in the
provinces. It was a pretty street, with trees peering over
garden walls, and small, old-fashioned villas with finicky
glass verandas. At night, the sound of footsteps on the side-
walks was so seldom heard as to seem almost startling.

What could ever happen to us? What could happen to

Paris? It had come out of the war practically unscathed, it was there to last, and to laugh and be happy forever, or so we thought. This feeling of security coming so soon after the false alarm of the preceding June is well nigh impossible to convey: it was the result of wishful thinking, I suppose, the wishful thinking of millions of Parisians who wanted to lead a quiet life in their beautiful city. No doubt we were living in a fool's paradise, but while it lasts, a fool's paradise is a mighty pleasant place to be in!

I wrote the concluding chapters of *Adrienne Mesurat* during the month of October and took the manuscript to the rue Garancière. Having left a typewritten copy of my novel on my publisher's desk, I crossed the courtyard of the old Hôtel de Sourdéac and deposited another copy in the hands of M. Le Grix, who had asked to publish it in his magazine, the *Revue Hebdomadaire* already referred to. And thus was my business attended to that day. I wonder what I did when I walked away from the rue Garancière. Not having kept a diary at the time, I do not know. Most probably I dawdled along the rue Bonaparte, looking at the bookstores, and no doubt refreshed myself with several *éclairs* at Poiré-Blanche, on the Boulevard Saint-Germain.

As I write these words, in a New England home, with a view of the White Mountains out of the window, and the latest news of the war in the Ukraine still lurking somewhere at the back of my mind, I cannot help wondering whether I am writing my own story or someone else's, someone I have known very well and have not seen for many years. It seems so strange not to be in Paris. . . . The White Mountains are beautiful through the summer haze, and there is something very kindly about this old house I am in, with its funny little casements and its prim little chintz curtains, but no sooner have I written the name of the Boulevard Saint-Germain than I find myself walking in the shade of the familiar chestnut trees, or down some of those old streets that have seen the invader march by so many times and have so many times outlived him.

A writer, when he is not actually engaged in writing a book, has a considerable amount of time on his hands. While he works, he seems to work harder than anyone else, but when he is not busy, he becomes what the French call a *flâneur*, an idler. O beautiful profession! To write the books one really wants to write, and to find it moreover possible to stroll through the streets of a city like Paris! I have wasted much time in strolling through streets and am glad of it. No one ever has strolled with greater pleasure than I. In those days, I seemed to discover something new and exciting in every street, and if there was not anything new or exciting in the streets, well, it still was Paris. At times, to be sure, a slight feeling of boredom came over me during these solitary walks, but boredom of a certain quality is one of the symptoms of happiness, of that quiet, everyday happiness which so many of us have lost. I caught myself yawning at the book-stalls along the Seine, simply because my eye had fallen so many times on worn-out copies of Voltaire's *Henriade*, that dull poem, or on Buffon's *Natural History*, or on *leste* eighteenth century drawings such as: *"Ma chemise brûle!"*, *"Il a la serrure, mais j'ai la clef!"* and Fragonard's well-known *Verrou*. But looking up, I would see the river gleaming through the leaves of the most beautiful plane trees in Paris, and the row of houses at the end of the island, or the solemn windows of the Louvre, and suddenly my heart went out to everything I saw, and I felt proud of my city.

As I look back on those days, it strikes me that I led an extraordinarily quiet life, a life which, in the eyes of most people, might have seemed dull, yet I can think of no period during which I was happier. I was never much given to going into what is called *le monde*. The thought of entering a drawing room and speaking to strange people was, on the contrary, so distasteful to me that such an experience amounted almost to an ordeal. I felt gauche and unhappy with those I did not know well and would have been quite contented to live forever in a small circle of intimate friends with whom I could speak as freely as I wished. However, some very pleasant friendships were, so to speak, forced upon me by circumstances.

It was at about this time that I met André Gide. Mr. Jacques Schiffrin, a Russian who was in the publishing business in Paris and to whom I had given the MS of a story, had asked me to lunch at his flat in the neighborhood of Montparnasse. His first wife, a brilliant and well-known pianist, was present, and Gide. Although I had already had occasion to see the latter, we had never yet spoken to each other, and I felt a little uneasy. The only books of his I had read at the time were *L'Immoraliste* and *La Porte Etroite*, and I feared that my ignorance as to his more important works would appear in the course of the conversation; but to my intense relief, I soon realized that, in spite of his literary reputation, André Gide was as reserved a person as I had ever met and certainly not one to talk shop in connection with his own books. He listened intently to what was said and asked questions which were extraordinarily to the point. His manner suggested a certain degree of self-consciousness; he had a way of clearing his throat whenever a lull occurred in the conversation, and I really believe that, strange as it may seem, he felt as shy as I did.

He wore a thick homespun suit which gave him an odd, tourist-like appearance, and for some reason this seemed totally out of keeping with his intellectual cast of features. It was as if his efforts to dress as simply as possible succeeded in making him only more conspicuous by an indefinable contrast between his face and the coarse material he wore. His eyes were the blackest I had ever seen, but what made them more remarkable was their quality of depth and intensity of expression; most people's eyes wander away into space every now and then, but his were ever present and attentive to the point of making one feel almost uncomfortable.

I forget what we talked about that day, except that he mentioned my last novel (*The Closed Garden*) which he had just read; with unusual intuition he referred to a certain passage, pointing out that no other page in the book could have given me more trouble. I listened with amazement; the page he had in mind had nothing at all remarkable about it, being simply a transition from one subject to another, but, as Gide had guessed, I had greatly labored over it. I cannot help thinking that he felt rather pleased with himself when he saw the look of surprise on my face.

Several days went by and he sent me his last book (*Le Journal des Faux-Monnayeurs*). By way of thanking him, I asked him to have dinner with me. As he has mentioned that evening at some length in his diary, I shall not say much about it; in later years, we often referred to it with amusement for several reasons which, if I remember well, he omitted in his account. Both of us were extremely reserved. We had dinner at Prunier's in the avenue Victor Hugo. ("Prunier!" I can still hear the note of surprise and ever so slight disapproval as he read the name of that famous restaurant over the door). After which we walked up to the Etoile and down the Champs-Elysées as far as a new café called the Lido, the entrance to which was in a covered gallery where people strolled rather aimlessly, looking at the shop windows or listening to the strains of a small orchestra. It happened that a red Indian was, that evening, the unwilling object of attraction in the gallery. What he was doing there, I do not know, but he immediately caught Gide's eye who found him *"vraiment très curieux"* with those feathers in his hair, and we followed him with the rest of the crowd. Perhaps I should have mentioned sooner that Gide himself was dressed in such a way as to arouse the curiosity of the passersby: he wore a long dark cape which made him look like a shepherd and a strange little cloth hat the brim of which he had pulled down over his eyes. Whether or not he considered this an inconspicuous way of dressing, I have never been able to make out, but the center of interest quickly passed from the red Indian to my companion and it was not long before I realized that Gide had unconsciously "stolen the show" from the American aborigine. This he never knew, nor will he mind my mentioning it here, should this book ever fall into his hands. Having satisfied his curiosity and unwittingly afforded much pleasure to the crowd of onlookers, he suggested having a drink at the Lido where he and I had never been.

We went down a staircase and found ourselves in a

Memories of Happy Days

large room full of rather smartly dressed people who sat at little tables around a long swimming pool. A glance at the place and a glance at Gide were enough to make me understand that he did not like the Lido. He obviously thought it pretentious and noisy, and so it was; nevertheless, we sat down and ordered some ices. An elaborate *fête de nuit* was in progress as we appeared. A program informed us that we were supposed to be in Venice towards 1750, and sure enough there was a gondola wreathed with roses in the middle of the pool, and in the gondola sat a masked lady who sang a barcarolle and made night hideous with her yowling; she was accompanied by a gentleman in white satin who thrummed a mandolin; soft lights illuminated this dreary scene.

I could not help grinning at the strangeness of it all, but Gide looked very somber and after a few efforts to carry on a *sotto voce* conversation, we both lapsed into a disapproving silence. Following the barcarolle, the lady *sang* one of Chopin's most hackneyed nocturnes, and Gide, who had always been a great admirer of that composer, groaned audibly. Being his guest I was careful not to give the slightest sign of impatience and he may have thought that I was enjoying myself, so on we stayed until at last, having consumed our ices over which we dawdled as long as we could, we suddenly and simultaneously became aware that we were both very tired, and left the Lido forever.

Memories of Happy Days. Such was the first evening I ever spent with André Gide. As I went home, I could not help regretting that, having been almost four hours in the company of one of the few great writers of our time, I had found so little to say, and I feared that I would not see him again for a long time, but in this I was wrong.

Adrienne Mesurat had a favorable reception in France and I frankly admit that I was overjoyed. No matter what authors may say to the contrary, success is more gratifying at the beginning of one's career than later, when excitement has been taken out of life by a long series of disappointments. The generosity with which my book was reviewed by French critics is one of the happy memories of my youth; I felt that my optimism was now justified to a certain degree and that I could face the future with greater confidence than I had ever known; but a heavy blow was about to strike me.

Early in the summer of 1927, my father died. He had been ailing for some time, but what really killed him was inaction, or perhaps what Charles Péguy once said of man in general was more particularly true of my father: he did not die of a disease, he died of his whole life, and his life had been a long life of hard work. He was the kindest and most considerate of fathers, and I had great reason to mourn him, but it took a number of years and a much greater ex-

Memories of Happy Days

perience of life than I had then for me to realize that he was one of the best men I had ever known. When I was a boy, I took it for granted that all men were as honest as he was and had as great a heart; I had much to learn.

One morning in November of that same year, I was called to the phone by my agent, Mr. William Bradley, who spoke to me for a few minutes. I had little to say, and having received his message, returned to my room where I sat on my bed. It was a dark room, very simply furnished, and I was so familiar with it as to know every crack in the floor and every tear in the wallpaper, but that morning it looked very strange and I had the curious feeling that I was not quite the same person when I came back into my room as when I had left it to answer the phone. Only a few minutes before, I was vaguely worried about my rent and how to meet my daily expenses. Now, there was no cause to worry about such things any more. *Adrienne Mesurat*, translated into English as *The Closed Garden*, had been chosen as the Book of the Month, which meant that, for years to come, I was to be free from any financial night-mare; I could write the books I wanted to write and could write them in peace.

During the next half hour, I was silent, trying to take in what had happened. Anyone else would probably have danced with joy, but I was stunned. And I regretted that

Memories of Happy Days this had not come a little sooner and that my father had not known about it.

New York, April 1942.